PIOTR WITKOWSKI

OPERATION MARKET GARDEN PARATROOPERS

MEANS OF TRANSPORT OF THE 1ST (POLISH) INDEPENDENT PARACHUTE BRIGADE 1941–1945

vol. 3

To my son Piotr and paratroopers of the 1st Independent Parachute Brigade

STRATUS

Published in Poland in 2017
by STRATUS sp.j.
Skr. Poczt. 123,
27-600 Sandomierz 1
e-mail: office@mmpbooks.biz
www.stratusbooks.pl

for
MMPBooks,
e-mail: office@mmpbooks.biz
© 2017 MMPBooks.
http://www.mmpbooks.biz

**ISBN
978-83-65281-75-3**

Editor in chief
Roger Wallsgrove

Editorial Team
Bartłomiej Belcarz
Robert Pęczkowski
Artur Juszczak

Colour Plates
Andrzej Gliński

Translation
Jarosław Dobrzyński

DTP
Stratus sp. j.

Printed by
Drukarnia Diecezjalna,
ul. Żeromskiego 4,
27-600 Sandomierz
www.wds.pl
marketing@wds.pl

PRINTED IN POLAND

TABLE OF CONTENTS

CHAPTER I
MEANS OF TRANSPORT
OF THE 1ST IPB

In its wartime history the 1st Independent Parachute Brigade used a broad range of transport, necessary for proper training and achieving combat readiness and performing combat tasks efficiently. The idea of adapting equipment for indigenous and Polish parachute units formed in Great Britain evolved with the British gaining experience in this field. Therefore types of vehicles used by the paratroopers were undergoing a similar process, from the phase of adaptation of current equipment to development of vehicles dedicated for airdropping along with parachute troops. As time went on and the situation on the frontline was changing, especially when the Allies gained air supremacy and numerical superiority on the Western Front, some earlier solutions proved ineffective, thus they were supported or replaced by others. This concerns for instance the use of Welbike folding motorcycles, which were intended as vehicles airdropped on the battlefield for subunits attached to unit headquarters. Military superiority allowed their replacement by better, but unsuitable for airdropping, heavier motorcycles, which were transported only aboard gliders.

The history of formation of the 1st IPB and achieving full combat readiness was directly associated with the condition of its transport column, and with the range of means of transport used by it. It should be remembered that the period in which the unit's "to be or not to be" was decided, which was influenced by lack of replenishments of enlisted men,[1] left a significant stamp on the quality and quantity of equipment supplied by the British, which they themselves did not have in overabundance. From the beginning of 1944 it was also influenced by the uncompromising attitude of the commander of the 1st IPB, Col./Gen. Sosabowski, who did not accept the use of the Brigade for tasks other than support of an uprising in occupied Poland. Only the British ultimatum, to which the Polish government in exile yielded, resulting in transfer of the Brigade under British command, resulted in a rapid influx of equipment, including transport, to the 1st IPB. Unfortunately it was after the opening of the second front in the West, when the decisions about the use of the Polish unit in an airborne assault operation were changing overnight. The specific merger of the equipment already possessed by the Brigade with the equipment being already supplied caused differences from the inventories of the British parachute brigades, the organization of which was the pattern for the Polish unit, hence the differences.

Another fact which influenced the difference was the guaranteed use of the 1st IPB in major Allied airborne assault operationa only in the second wave, after landing of British and American units. This was quickly reflected in the number of transport gliders given to the Polish unit, the number of which diminished from 100, expected by the command of the 1st IPB, to 35[2]. This fact is apparent in analysis of the Brigade's documents from the pre-battle period, in which the planned numbers and types of means of transport prepared for the battle in mid-July 1944 was cut down during the immediate preparations for Operation Market Garden.

---

1   Until the battle of Arnhem in September 1944 the Polish brigade had not reached full complement, the best proof of which is the disbandment of the 4th Parachute Battalion, existing in skeletal form, the soldiers of which reinforced the remaining three battalions. Despite this the squads in these subunits did not reach British complements, i.e. 10 soldiers. Usually they numbered 6-8 paratroopers.

2   J. H. Dyrda, *Udział I Polskiej Samodzielnej Brygady Spadochronowej w desancie wojsk powietrznych w Arnhem we wrześniu 1944 r.*, Bellona, Issue 10, Łódź 1946, pp. 697-698.

UNPOWERED VEHICLES OF THE 1ST IPB

TROLLEY AND HANDCART AIRBORNE CARTS

Immediately after landing the paratrooper was usually unaided, in respect of transport of equipment and armament. Airdropped group equipment, ammunition supplies and weapons had to be taken from the drop zone immediately. This often was done under enemy fire, as it was at Driel. Therefore a means of transport allowing the paratrooper to take a considerable load of equipment or even an entire container was necessary.

Left: Folded trolley. Tow ropes are visible (Wikipedia).
Right: Polish paratroopers unfolding a trolley retrieved from a container in the drop zone. (MIT)

Such a handy device was the lightweigh folding airborne cart, called a trolley. The design resembled a wheelbarrow and the load container was made of canvas, reinforced by sewn-on canvas straps. The trolley was pushed by the soldier, for which two handles, as in a wheelbarrow, were used. It had two wheels with inflatable tyres. The entire construction could be folded thanks to joints secured with knobs, hence its usefulness, because a folded trolley was loaded on top of the container's content and after having been taken out and deployed could be used to quickly move the container with its contents. Thanks to this paratrooper subunits equipped with trolleys could pick up the equipment in the drop zone and go to area safe from enemy fire and retrieve the needed equipment and weapons from the containers there.

If the weight of the trolley was too heavy for a single paratrooper or the terrain was rough, e.g. a sandy road, he could be aided by two others, who pulled the trolley, using hemp or sisal ropes attached to the its forward bar. In the 1st IPB it was mostly the squads of the Airborne Engineer Company and communication teams who were equipped with the trolleys, although in the beginning of Brigade's existence they were widely used in the subunits, being in fact the only handy mean of transport.

There was also a larger version of the trolley, used for carrying equipment from the drop zone. It could be also used as a light trailer for a Jeep, the Airborne/Infantry Folding Handcart.

It was similar to carts widely used in agriculture for transporting produce, with a drawbar. The difference was that while an agricultural cart was a fixed construction, the airborne cart could be dismantled, having folding axles with wheels, which allowed for reduction of the cart's dimensions. As in case of the much smaller trolley, the soldier pushing the cart could be supported by two others, pulling the cart with ropes attached to the cart's frame.

Polish paratroopers using a Handcart. It is hard to determine whether this photograph was taken during the battle. (IPMS)

4

British paratroopers marching with a Handcart. Commemoration of the 60th anniversary of the Battle of Arnhem in 2004.

Analysis of the iconographic material from the early days of the Brigade as well as from later years does not indicate that the Handcarts were often used in the 1st IPB, which was caused by the possibility of delivering them to the battlefield virtually only with the glider component and this matter was always uncertain (the number of gliders assigned to the Brigade) because the Brigade did not have its own glider brigade and was dependent on the British. Certainly they were not popular, because although they could be folded, they did not fit into drop containers. However, in the battle the 1st IPB used mainly light airborne trailers for Jeeps, of much more robust construction and hence load capacity. The Handcarts were used at Arnhem on a much wider scale by British airborne units, as archive photographs show.

AIRBORNE BICYCLE

The British arms manufacturer – Birmingham Small Arms Company (BSA) – was founded as early as 1861. Apart from many other famous products, for historians interested in the history of parachute forces it usually associated with motorcycles, and primarily with a bicycle intended for these forces – the folding and airdropped BSA "Paratrooper".

The company's tradition of producing bicycles for the military dates back to the Boer War, when BSA bicycles were used by British infantrymen to travel across vast expanses of the Transvaal. Its characteristic feature, distinguishing it from other bicycles, were grips enabling transporting a rifle so that the cyclist had both hands free[3].

The BSA company continued this tradition during the First World War and thereafter, when in large infantry units of European armies cyclist platoons began to be formed.

BSA airborne bicycle. On the tubes of the frame two joints are secured by screws with butterfly nuts, used for folding the frame for transport or airdropping. (MWP)

---

3 https://bsamuseum.wordpress.com/military-bicycles-in-the-boer-war/ – access: 1.05.2015.

5

Paratroopers with BSA airborne bicycles in 1944, before the battle.

Parachute units, forming at the beginning of the next war, quickly faced the problem of mobility of their subunits, especially messengers and liaison. While the use of motorcycles and other vehicles opened broad possibilities, transport of them complicated the situation. Gliders were necessary to transport them, which however was expensive and often impossible. While the parachute infantry could land virtually on any open area, landing grounds for gliders had much higher requirements.

In order not to paralyse the command system in parachute subunits, which anyway was prone to difficulties from many directions and dependent on a bit of luck, it was decided to develop a parachute bicycle, lightweight thanks to

Folded airborne bicycle. (Embacher-Collection/Bernhard Angerer)

BSA bicycle folded and prepared for airdrop. Small cargo parachute dedicated for this bicycle is attached to the wheels. (Embacher-Collection/Bernhard Angerer)

BSA Airborne Folding Paratroopers Bicycle, model 1944, differing from the earlier one in having single under-saddle tube. (Embacher-Collection/Bernhard Angerer)

a folding frame and small size construction. So the bicycle for airborne units, the BSA Airborne Bicycle, was developed in 1942[4].

The bicycle was a typical men's model of that time, but its frame was made of double steel tubes, separate but joined together with welded steel crosspieces. The frame was eye-shaped and using two butterfly nuts it was possible to fold it to the right so that there was no necessity to remove the chain, which was always stretched between two sprockets. The wheel arms of the sprocket formed the lettering BSA.

---

4   https://bsamuseum.wordpress.com/1942-ww2-bsa-airborne-bicycle-early-twin-tube-model/ – access: 1.05.2015.

Phases of unfolding the BSA bicycle. The paratrooper unfolds the frame, locks it with butterfly nuts and the bicycle is ready for use. (A. Dzimira)

The bicycle was devoid of any redundant parts, such as mudguards, lights (a metal grip on the handlebar post, to attach a flashlight, was left), bell and even pedals, whose role was taken over by their axles (but initially the bicycle had pedals).

Under the leather spring-cushioned saddle a leather case for bicycle wrenches was suspended. A characteristic feature, distinguishing 1942 models, was double seat tube. In models of the later pattern, produced 1942-1945, it was single, but of larger diameter, to accommodate the seat post. The bicycle had also a pump attached to the seat tube, in the earlier model inside the frame and in the later model outside, facing the rear wheel. The bicycle was also equipped with a canvas bag, suspended on the top tube inside the frame on standard straps. It enabled carrying additional equipment. The bicycle had also front and rear wheel brakes and the handlebar was fitted with rubber grips with a stamped company logo[5].

The second pattern of the bicycle, produced in 1942-1945 (*BSA Airborne Folding Paratroopers Bicycle*), often called "para bike", was different virtually only in respect of the seat tube. All models were painted dark military green.

Airborne bicycles lost their significance after being replaced by motorcycles and Jeeps, but the possibility of taking them aboard the airplane with the paratroopers enabled using them in the drop zone.

Riding this bicycle was not a thing to dream of because the vehicle was a simplified, if not primitive, design. The reduction ratio, i.e. coupling of sprockets, was typical for that time, making the bicycle more useful for riding a paved road, not on rough terrain. It also had no luggage rack, which would certainly be useful for a paratrooper, always heavily loaded with equipment and weapons.

Soldiers of the Airborne Signals Company at the airfield prepare a folding bicycle for airdrop before the departure for Operation "Market Garden". (IPMS)

The 1st IPB had a large number of folding bicycles in its inventory[6]. According to wartime complement of the unit, its subunits had in total 197 folding bicycles, according to following list: Headquarters – 5, Military Police platoon – 10, field post – 2, four parachute battalions – 4 x 20, Signals Company – 10, Medical Company – 18, Airborne (Light) Artillery Battery[7] – 62[8].

Before the departure for Operation Market Garden the number of airborne bicycles was 115, according to the list made by Col. Jan Kamiński on 19 September 1944[9]. However, a smaller number was taken for combat due to the limited number of C-47 aircraft assigned for transporting the 1st IPB.

---

5   *Ibidem.*
6   Moreover, the headquarters of parachute battalions (mainly command companies) had also unfolding bicycles – 13 per battalion. See: *1.Samodzielna Brygada Spadochronowa. Organizacja wojenna* (rok 1943), IPMS, A.V.20/31/15 – doc. 5,12.
7   Development of Brigade's artillery into Light Artillery Squadron and Anti-tank Artillery Squadron was done on the strength of the order L.dz.242/Tjn.Org.44, of 28.03.1944; 1.Samodzielna Brygada Spadochronowa. Zarys rozwoju organi-zacyjnego, IPMS, sygn. A.V.20/31/15 – doc.1, p. 2.
8   1.Samodzielna Brygada Spadochronowa. Organizacja wojenna, IPMS, A.V.20/31/15 – doc. 5, p. 28.
9   J. Kamiński, *Operacja wojsk alianckich "Market Garden"*, WBBH, sign. XII/12/89.

PAINT SCHEMES AND MARKINGS OF VEHICLES OF THE 1ST IPB

Vehicles assigned to the 1st Polish Corps in Scotland were painted in accordance with regulations of the British Army in a single military colour, referred to as Olive Green Drab[10] or another, more frequently applied to larger vehicles, referred to as Bronze Green[11].

When the units of this Corps entered combat in the West European theatre, the paint scheme was supplemented by additional camouflage. The motorcycles were left in their original paint scheme, without camouflage, but automobiles, from passenger cars used by the military to large trucks, had black camouflage blotches applied.

The camouflage patterns had two shapes: either irregular smudges, covering bodies and canvas hoods of the cars, or oval blots, resembling ears of the most popular cartoon character of that time, Mickey Mouse, hence the frequent description of this camouflage pattern by this name. The camouflage pattern was two-colour, the basic orifinal green of the car's body and the second black or earth brown of the blotches.

The main purpose of camouflaging vehicles was blurring the regular lines of the vehicle's silhouette remembered by observer's eyes. Here the camouflage pattern of irregular smudges was often used. Another British concept was reversal of intensity of illumination of most the exposed parts of the vehicle by the sun – cab tops, bonnets and upper surfaces of truck bed tarpaulin covers. Therefore, in order to change the intensity of their illumination and hence change the silhouette of the vehicle (optical illusion principle), these surfaces were painted black, with the splotches reaching upper parts of side surfaces or covering the entire surfaces. The camouflage was applied with a paintbrush or paint gun.

Analysis of archive photographs concerning the 1st IPB shows unambiguously that heavy vehicles of this unit (trucks) were usually painted using darkening of upper body surfaces by the "mickey mouse" camouflage pattern. When the unit joined operations in mainland Europe in September 1944 (the naval component – trucks and other vehicles – departed as early as 15 August 1944) the vehicles sent to France and then Netherlands were camouflaged by nets, covering the tarpaulins and sides of the truck beds.

Smaller cars, except for Willys/Jeeps, were painted in irregular black or less often earth brown smudges over all the body.

1ST POLISH CORPS INSIGNIA

The 1st Polish Corps in Scotland had its own insignia. It was a white circle with a wing on a black background. The order required to be placed on:

Left front mudguard, or on vehicles having no mudguards, on the left side,

At the rear of the vehicle on the left mudguard or in a clearly visible place on the left side,

On vehicles featuring a windshield, the badge was to be placed in the lower left corner of the windshield,

On motorcycles, on the left side of the fuel tank[12]

1st Polish Corps insignia, in force from December 1940 till the end of 1943 and example of placing it on a vehicle of the 1st IPB. (JD)

---

10 Applied on bicycles, Welbike motorcycles or PIAT anti-tank weapons.

11 J. Bouchery, *The British Soldier. From D-Day to VE-Day*, vol.2, Paris 1999, p. 126.

12 J. Murgrabia, *Symbole wojskowe Polskich Sił Zbrojnych na Zachodzie 1939-1946*, Warsaw 1990, p. 112.

The relevant order was issued on 12 December 1940 and was in force until the end of 1943[13]. However, at least in the 1st IPB it was painted only until 1943-44, when it was abandoned. This was probably because the unit obtained its own insignia (the Parachute Badge), which was painted on all vehicles previously marked with the insignia of the 1st Corps. New vehicles arriving at the unit had not had the Corps insignia applied, only the unit badge.

VEHICLE GROUP CLASSIFICATION SYMBOLS

Each registration number was preceded by the appropriate letter, denoting its affiliation to a specific group. This is the list of vehicle groups:

A – ambulances
C – motorcycles
E – engineer vehicles
F – armoured cars, including wheeled ones
H – wheeled tractors
M – passenger cars, staff cars, some lightly armoured scout cars, Jeeps,
L – open-bed trucks with load capacity in excess of 750 kg, some lightly armoured scout cars,
P – amphibious cars
S – self-propelled, armoured, tracked guns
T – tanks and other armoured, tracked combat vehicles (e.g. Universal Carrier),
V – vans, closed body vehicles (workshop and maintenance trucks)
X – trailers
Z – trucks with load capacity below 750 kg, half-track and wheeled armoured personnel carriers[14].

REGISTRATION NUMBER (WAR DEPARTMENT NUMBER)

Each vehicle had to display on both sides its registration number, which was in fact its record number in the British Army, part of which were the Polish units[15]. These numbers, preceded by an appropriate letter, comprised up to 7 digits.

In the 1st IPB they were painted white, although at least one photograph of a Brigade's Jeep shows that the number was painted in light blue, as on the Jeeps of the British 1st Airborne Division.

These numbers were usually painted on the upper parts of the doors or on both sides of the bonnet. Sometimes on Jeeps and artillery tractor trucks the number was painted on the tailgate or on the back of the car. On motorcycles the number was painted on both sides of the fuel tank.

Method of painting War Department Numbers on trucks belonging to the 1st IPB. (P. Wybraniec)

13 *Ibidem*, p. 111.
14 A. A. Kamiński, T. Szczerbicki, *Pojazdy Polskich Sił Zbrojnych na Zachodzie 1939-1947*, Gdańsk 2008, p. 323.
15 *Ibidem*, p. 326.

BRIDGE CLASSIFICATION NUMBERS

Bridge classification numbers indicated axle load, which was important when crossing bridges. It enabled the soldiers controlling the traffic to assess quickly whether a given vehicle is able to safely cross the bridge, often improvised, or not. In such instances the vehicle was usually directed to a place where its passage would not damage the bridge.

They were in the shape of a yellow disc, 22.8 cm[16] in diameter, within which a proper designation in the form of an Arabic numeral, as below, was painted. The numbers were either painted on vehicle bodies or made in the form of a plate, screwed on parts of the body or light. They were not painted on motorcycles and bicycles.

Bridge classification numbers were painted only on the front of vehicles, usually on the right bumper or right side of the body. On Jeeps the numbers were usually painted under the windscreen, in the middle.

Bridge classification numbers used for marking types of vehicles[17]

1 – motorcycles, small passenger cars, Jeeps
2 – Jeeps, larger passenger cars, light pick-up cars
3/2 – Jeeps with trailers.
3 – heavy passenger cars, sometimes 15-cwt trucks
4 – Morris-Commercial 30-cwt GS truck
5 – most 15-cwt trucks
6 – most 30-cwt trucks

The same type of vehicle, a Dodge L60, with different bridge classification numbers. The photos are taken before the end of the war and after, during the occupation of Germany. (RN)

---

16 J. Bouchery *op. cit., pp*. 125,127. The regulation size was not always observed.
17 D.E. Jane, British military transport, London 1978, p. 4.

11

Bridge classification marking, marked by an arrow, painted on the background of the body colour. The number is painted in black on the truck's body, within a yellow circle instead of the yellow disc. (IPMS)

7 – sometimes 3-ton 4x2, Bedford QLT Troopers trucks
8 – 5-ton wheeled trucks with trailers
9 – most 3-ton 4x2, 4x4, 6x4 trucks.

WARTIME MARKINGS OF 1ST IPB SUBUNITS

Within military units marking of individual subunits was often used, since it facilitated recognition of the subunits, soldiers and equipment assignment. It was particularly important in parachute units, whose character of operations (air dropping or deployment behind enemy lines aboard gliders) often was and still is the cause of dispersal of subunits and equipment throughout the drop or landing zone and beyond. For better organization after landing subunit markings were used to easily direct individual soldiers, transported equipment and weapons to places of gathering after landing.

In the 1st IPB individual subunits obtained numbers, differing in colour. The dimensions of the plates were theoretically standardized and compliant to British regulations, but in reality they could have different dimensions. This was usually because of the characteristic features of vehicle designs, particularly cars. External measurements of the plates used in British units and the Brigade were 24.14 cm x 21.6 cm with the digits 15.4 cm tall[18].

Plates with markings of 1st subunits (right) and method of placing them on a vehicle belonging to the 1st IPB. (MWP/MS)

NATIONALITY MARKINGS

On all vehicles of the Polish Armed Forces in the West the nationality marking was painted. It was a white, rimless oval with black capital letters PL. These markings were made by various methods, from painting with a template to freehand, which the following archive photographs show. Both the shape and size were not standardized, although there was care that the marking retained common features and proportions.

18 J. Bouchery, *op. cit.*, pp. 125-127.

In the left photo a hand-painted nationality marking is visible. The combination of it with the unit insignia, the Parachutist Badge, is also quite unusuall. At right, a stencilled "PL" marking. Its size was suitable for the type of vehicle. (RN)

PARACHUTIST BADGE – UNIT EMBLEM

Apart from painting and camouflaging, the vehicles were also marked. From 1941 major units of the 1st Polish Corps in Scotland were allowed to place their emblems on their vehicles. The emblem was the Parachutist Badge without crest, painted in white. There were two methods of painting: in a white box or directly on the vehicle's body. The latter method was more widely used after the war, during the occupation of Germany.

The emblem was painted in various places, depending on the type of vehicle, but there also were differences in its location among vehicles of the same type.

The chief principle of applying the Parachutist Badge was painting it on the front and back of the vehicle, initially excluding motorcycles from this principle, but later (during occupation of Germany) it also concerned them.

Unit insignia plate of a vehicle assigned to the Brigade's HQ. Original preserved at Polish Army Museum and graphic image of the stencil.

Parachutist Badges painted on mudguards of motorcycles. Post-war period. (RN)

AIR RECOGNITION MARKINGS

Beginning in 1944, when the Allied invasion of the Continent from the British Isles was being prepared, the American white five-pointed star was adopted as an air recognition marking for all Allied vehicles. Initially only American military vehicles were marked with this symbol, but from the beginning of preparations for Operation Overlord it became a common marking for all Allied vehicles fighting on the Western front.

The markings were painted on car bonnets, cab tops and lateral surfaces, although there without the outline. It could be easily seen by friendly aircraft, which were expected to win air superiority quickly, which indeed happened.

Polish Armed Forces in the West usually painted the star inverted on their vehicles, which additionally distinguished Polish vehicles. The stars were usually stencilled.

An example of American stars painted on a 1ˢᵗ IPB's truck. Stars on the sides are inverted and painted with a homemade stencil, which the lack of proportions of the figure shows. (RN)

PERSONAL MARKINGS

In the 1ˢᵗ IPB, with strict discipline under the command of Col./Gen Stanisław Sosabowski, there was no habit of marking vehicles with personal emblems or names. This art was developed later, particularly during the occupation of Germany after May 1945. However, there were some exceptions. Archive photos depict a Brigade's Universal Carrier with an emblem in the form of a small parachute. Later, during the occupation of Germany the regulations were liberated and allowed painting of individual names on vehicles.

*Examples of applying personal markings on vehicles of the 1ˢᵗ IPB. **Left:** Universal Carrier – circa 1942 (IPMS).*
***Right:** the fuel bowser – naval component of Operation Market Garden. A four-leaf clover is visible in the back of the bowser.*

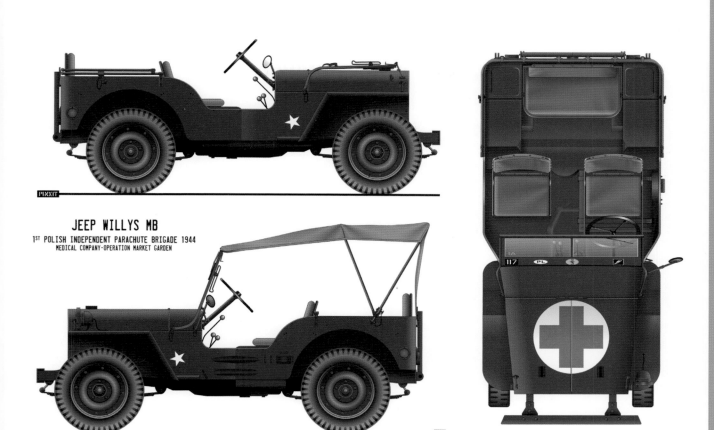

JEEP WILLYS MB
1ST POLISH INDEPENDENT PARACHUTE BRIGADE 1944
MEDICAL COMPANY-OPERATION MARKET GARDEN

MAX. SPEED
40 MPH

CAUTION
LEFT HAND
DRIVE
NO SIGNAL

Geneva Red Cross Symbol	1st IPB emblem	Vehicle Unit Marking	Bridge Classification Number	Nationality marking	Allied Star	War Department Number

Paint and marking scheme of a Willys Jeep of the Airborne Medical Company during Operation Market Garden in September 1944.

Personal markings in form of female names "Heluś" and "Emilia" painted on the bumpers. (RN)

Markings of 1ˢᵗ IPB vehicles[19]
(see opposite page)
1. Plate of a vehicle assigned to 1ˢᵗ IPB headquarters
2. Parachutist Badge in non-divided box
3. Parachutist Badge in stencilled box
4. Parachutist Badge without box, painted on a vehicle's body
5. Simplified Parachutist Badge, without box, painted on the background of the vehicle's body colour.
6. Markings of vehicles assigned to individual subunits of the 1ˢᵗ IPB: 109 – headquarters
7. 109 on navy blue-white-navy blue background – Airborne Signals Company
8. 110 – 1ˢᵗ Parachute Battalion
9. 111 – 2ⁿᵈ Parachute Battalion
10. 112 – 3ʳᵈ Parachute Battalion
11. 113 – 4ᵗʰ Parachute Battalion
12. 114 – Light Artillery Squadron
13. 115 – Airborne Anti-tank Artillery Squadron
14. 116 – Airborne Engineer Company
15. 117 – Airborne Medical Company
16. 118 – Transport and Supply Company
17. War Department Number for a Jeep
18. War Department Number for a Universal Carrier
19. Bridge classification number for a Jeep with trailer and Jeep solo, painted on the body. Below: plate with bridge classi-fication number in form of a plaque screwed on the bumper and in a form painted on the body, without yellow back-ground filling the inside of the marking.
20. Nationality markings, stencilled and hand-painted, of various shapes and sizes.
21. Allied Forces recognition markings (American white star), painted on vehicles' doors: regulation one (proportional, rim-less), inverted, but stencilled one and hand-painted one. Below: Allied air recognition markings, stencilled on vehicles' bonnets and cab tops, various versions. On these surfaces stars in the complete version, with the rim, were painted.

---

19 Markings 1 and 6 – 16 are based on collections of the Polish Army Museum in Warsaw. The rest were made on the basis of archive photographs.

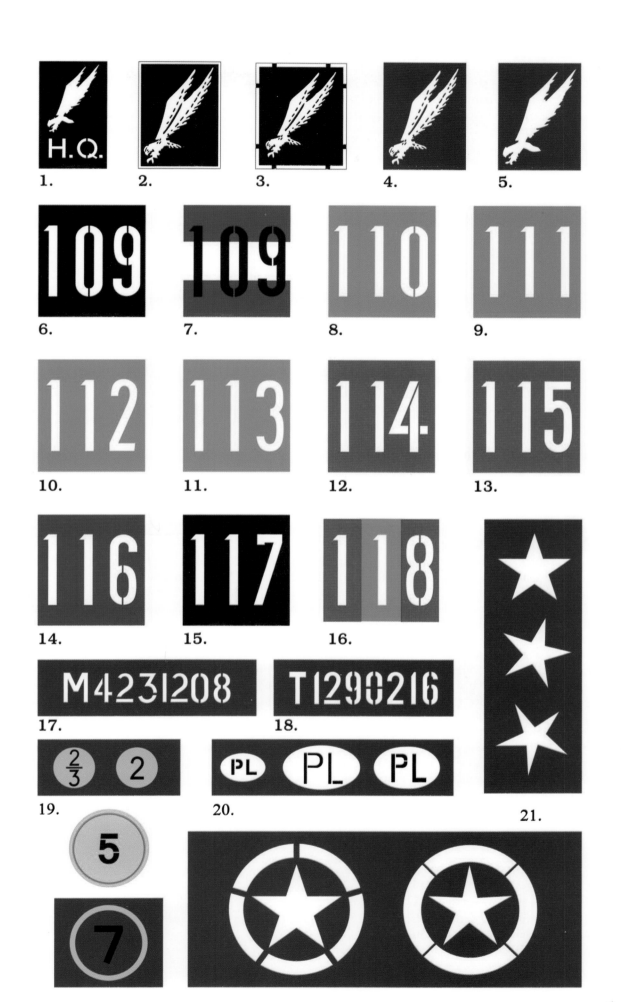

1. 2. 3. 4. 5.

6. 7. 8. 9.

10. 11. 12. 13.

14. 15. 16.

17. 18.

19. 20. 21.

MOTOR VEHICLES OF THE 1ST INDEPENDENT PARACHUTE BRIGADE

An independent unit, the purpose of which is combat in isolation from friendly forces, often in encirclement, being the spearhead of the forces, must have in its inventory all vehicles enabling it to conduct its assigned task and simply to function. The designs described below were characterized by particular usefulness for parachute units thanks to the possibility of deploying them to the battlefield either aboard gliders or by dropping them from aircraft carrying airborne infantry to the drop zones.

However, such a large unit as a brigade and so specific, because an airborne one, needed a diverse park of vehicles supporting it in combat. They had the task of supporting their own forces dropped on the battlefield, after having reached it immediately after a friendly armoured spearhead. During garrison service these vehicles bore the burden of carrying men and equipment during training and exercises.

Having two types of artillery, 75 mm calibre field gun and 57 mm calibre anti-tank artillery, the Brigade had to secure artillery tractors, preferably with crews. The British war potential in this field was not small, but rather unsophisticated, hence adaptation of current trucks of various load capacities and purpose. The park was complemented by specialized vehicles, such as fuel or water tankers, mobile canteens or ambulances, capable of carrying several heavily wounded soldiers at the same time.

The 1st Independent Parachute Brigade had a numerous and diverse vehicle park. It played its major role during garrison service, but a large part of it was intended to be an additional motorized component of the Brigade. In combat conditions it was carried within the 1st and 2nd naval component of the unit, deployed to the mainland by a fleet of transport ships.

The lists of vehicles from July[20] and September[21] 1944 allows us to know the number and types of vehicles that the 1st IPB had at its disposal at that time. This situation was changed when in 1945 the Brigade was re-organized, the losses were replenished and the strength was increased. The unit itself, due to impending conclusion of the war, was not to be used in an airborne operation, hence some equipment was replaced by new types, which gave the 1st IPB the form close to an independent motorized infantry brigade. In this form it was deployed by sea to the continent, where it saw the end of the war. As we know, it was not withdrawn, but instead deployed to the British occupation zone in Germany, where it stood on occupation duty along with the Polish 1st armoured Division of Gen. Stanisław Maczek in the district of Berrsenbrück [22].

The numbers and type of vehicles used in Germany also changed. The Brigade received other types of heavy motorcycles, American Studebaker trucks and even Universal Carrier light armoured tracked vehicles. The new equipment complemented or replaced the existing inventory. Here it would be advisable to present a list, based on documents and archive photographs, of all types of vehicles operated by the 1st IPB both during the pre-battle period (1941-44) and after the battle, until the return of the Brigade from occupation duties in Germany and disbandment of the Polish Armed Forces in the West in 1947.

"WELBIKE" FOLDING MOTORCYCLE

It was an amazing design, as were many others at that time, based on British technical thinking and following two principles, so important for Great Britain during this war – simplicity and economy. It deserves more thorough coverage.

The design was developed in 1942 for the needs of the British Special Operations Executive (SOE), one of the tasks of which was "setting Europe ablaze"[23] by supporting resistance movements in German-occupied countries by all available means. Hence the demand for a vehicle of small size for intelligence agents or partisans, that could be airdropped with the jumper into occupied territory. It would increase mobility of SOE agents or their local allies.

The motorcycle was designed by Harry Lester, an employee of the SOE research and development centre located near Welvyn[24], Hertfordshire, basing on the concept by Col. John Dolphin[25] from the same facility.

This unsophisticated design had its drawbacks, including a quite loud but underpowered engine. A disadvantage, that could cost the SOE agent his life, was the necessity of preparing the motorcycle to ride each time. It consisted of manual generating pressure in the fuel tank by hand-pumping the mixture (the engine had no fuel pump). Without it, starting the engine was impossible. This action had to be repeated after travelling a distance of around 10-15 miles[26].

Probably this factor became one of the reasons which in the opinion of SOE specialists made the vehicle unsuitable for use by intelligence agents. However, the design aroused the interest of decision makers of the British airborne forces, especially after having passed evaluation at a proving ground.

In 1942 airdropping trials with various containers were conducted. Final report from the trials indicated that the CLE[27] (also known as Mk.I.T) type container proved to be the optimal one. The motorcycle was dropped from a Wellington

---

20   *Urgent memorandum. Subject: "B" Vehicles*, IPMS, sign.: A.V.20/31/15 – doc. 23. See: Annex 1

21   J. Kamiński, *Operacja wojsk alianckich "Market Garden"*, WBBH, sign. XII/12/89. See: Annex 2

22   J. Rydel, *"Polska okupacja" w północno-zachodnich Niemczech 1945-1948*, Krakow 2000, p. 105.

23   The phrase used by British Prime Minister Winston Churchill in conversations with SOE leaders in 1940.

24   Hence the name Welbike – a merger of the first part of the township name Welwyn and the word "bike". See: http:Home.earthlink.net/flyboyken/id15.html – access: 24.09.2013.

25   A. Zasieczny, *Broń Wojska Polskiego 1939-1945. Wojska lądowe*, Warsaw 2006, p. 101.

26   *Ibidem*, p. 101

27   CLE – *Container Light Equipment*.

A British paratrooper on an Excelsior 98cc Welbike Mk I folding motorcycle.

Welbike motorcycle
ready for use and in
n airdrop container,
with handlebars and
seat folded. The load
compartment of the
container with the
motorcycle and cargo
parachute compart-
ment are visible.
1. CLE-type container
   – section,
2. Operating manual,
3. External markings
   on the container.

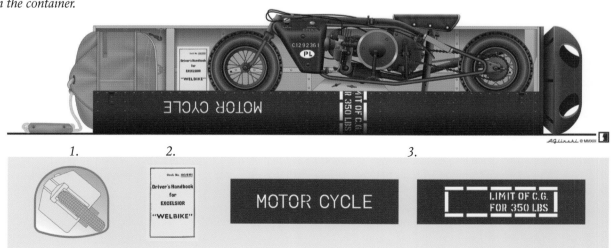

1.   2.   3.

Markings and rating plates placed on a Welbike motorcycle. Views of the motorcycle ready to ride and folded for stowing in airdrop container.

Engine: markings, manufacturer's logo, serial number

War Department Number and nationality marking

Manufacturer's logo

REMOVE PLUG BEFORE RUNNING. FILL SLOWLY TO 1/2" OF BASE OF HOLE REPLACE CAP TIGHTLY. USE PETROIL MIXTURE 16 PARTS PETROL 1 PART M220 OIL MIX THOROUGHLY

Markings on left fuel tank

REMOVE BEFORE FILLING, REPLACE AFTER. FILL SLOWLY TO BASE OF HOLE REPLACE TIGHTLY.

Markings on right fuel tank

aircraft flying at an altitude of 500 ft and speed of 130 mph[28]. Positive results of the evaluation led to the placing of an order for several thousand of these vehicles at the Excelsior Motor Co. Ltd factory in Birmingham[29].

As already mentioned, the vehicle was of small size. The total weight of the motorcycle with empty tanks was less than 32 kg (70 lbs). Range on one tank of 6.5 pints[30] of petrol and ¼ pint of oil[31] mixture was estimated to be less than 150 km (ca. 90 miles). The motorcycle attained a maximum speed of 30 mph (50 km/h)[32]. The fuel consumption was about 3 litres/100 km[33].

---

28   Attempts of dropping the motorcycle in Mk III container were not successful, because the vehicle could fit only when the tyres were deflated. This detail disqualified this type of container due to protracted preparation of the vehicle for use.

29   The number of examples produced from 1942 till the end of 1945 is estimated at 3,853. See: Zasieczny, *op. cit*, p. 101.

30   British volume unit, ca. 568 ml

31   *Maintenance Manual for Excelsior 98 cc. "Welbike"*, Book No. 101/EM1, p. 1. According to the rating plate on the engine the mixture of petrol and Castrol XL oil in proportion 16:1 was used. The recommended gear oil for the clutch was Castrol "D".

32   *Driver's Handbook for Excelsior "Welbike"*, Book No. 100/EMI, p. 1.

33   A. Zasieczny, *op. cit.*, p. 101.

The motorcycle prepared for locking in the airdrop container.

The frame was made of welded steel tubes, constituting the vehicle's skeleton. Bicycle-type handlebars had a clutch lever on the left end and throttle grip on the right end. To prevent hands slipping on the handlebars the grips were padded with thick canvas.

The size of the vehicle could be reduced on packing by unscrewing the screw on the top of the handlebars, which allowed folding handles. To fold it vertically the safety pin on the steel tube strut, holding it in an upright position, had to be unlocked. Then the handlebar was laid flat on the frame. A similar operation was conducted with the bicycle-type seat, sliding into a tube in the frame.

Immediately aft of the front wheel, on both sides of the frame, two separate fuel tanks were mounted, designed to be as small as possible. The tanks were connected with a fuel line. The fuel valve was located at the lowest point, below the carburettor. Opening it resulted in the mixture flowing into the carburettor. On the right tank a hand fuel pump and fuel tank vent were located[34]. The right tank was filled by pulling the hand pump, acting also as the fuel filler cap. The left tank also had a fuel inlet with automatic vent valve. The fuel tank capacity was 3.7 l[35]. The exhaust manifold was mounted conventionally at the bottom of the frame. The motorcycle had only a rear wheel brake.

Bicycle-type seat on spring, covered by black genuine or artificial leather, was adopted. The seat was mounted atop the steel tube seat post, which could be lowered for transport by sliding into the vertical under-seat tube of the frame.

The powerplant of the Welbike was a 98 cc two-stroke, single-cylinder, air-cooled, carburetted Villiers Junior engine[36], which was the central part of the frame.

The Welbike was designed to fit into a CLE type container, dropped onto the battlefield on a cargo parachute. To load the motorcycle into the container first the handlebars and seat had to be folded and then the motorcycle had to be placed in the container with the rear wheel pointing towards the outer bumper of the container, which was intended to minimize damage to the vehicle on landing. This method was the result of tests conducted with the motorcycle by SOE. The motorcycle stowed in the container was secured against moving inside with wooded blocks placed under the engine and at both wheels[37].

After landing the paratrooper had to find a container with white legend "Motor Cycle" in the drop zone and retrieve the motorbike. To shorten the procedure of engine startup the rider did not have to use the hand fuel pump because proper pressure was generated before loading the bike into containers, so between retrieval of the vehicle from the container to engine startup only a short time elapsed.

After having filled the tank with fuel and generated proper pressure with the hand pump in the fuel tanks, deployed the handlebar and seat, the rider had to open the fuel valve and "flood" the carburettor with fuel. Then, holding the

---

34   In archive photos differences in location of fuel inlets and tank vents are often visible.
35   Maintenance Manual for Excelsior 98 cc. "Welbike"…, p. 1.
36   A. Zasieczny, *op. cit.*, p. 101.
37   Dropping of solo motor cycle in containers. Report No.A.F.E.E./P.55…, c.3.

clutch handle with his left hand he opened the throttle twisting the grip and pushed the motorcycle, releasing the clutch and throttling. After startup the two-stroke engine ran at high RPM for about 30 seconds, receiving an increased mixture dose. Then the rider had to push the choke button on the carburettor, which caused the engine to throttle back to slower normal RPM. After having completed these operations, the rider could ride the bike.

To stop the engine, the rider had to twist the throttle grip towards himself, squeezing the clutch handle and then cut off the fuel supply with the fuel valve[38]. The motorcycle had small dimensions: length – 132.1 cm, width – 55.9 cm, height when ready for use – 78.1 cm[39].

Light weight of the vehicle (empty 32 kg) allowed the paratrooper to carry it over terrain obstacles – ditches, walls or fences – unaided. Although the Welbike was not a powerful motorcycle, it could easily carry a fully equipped paratrooper.

Riding this motorcycle certainly was not comfortable due to its small size and lack of shock absorbers. Hence after landing in rough terrain, often on a ploughed field, not being able to ride the motorcycle across it, soldiers abandoned them in the drop zone. The system of air-dropping troops and equipment separately often meant that dispersion was wide and the paratrooper had no opportunity or time to find the container with the motorcycle.

During Operation Market Garden British airborne units employed the latest system of troop and equipment transport, involving use of military gliders, although they usually carried heavier motorcycles, better suited for the battlefield than the Welbike.

Review of 1st IPB subunits. Largo House, 1943. (IPMS)

Polish paratroopers with Welbike motorcycles during a review. (IPMS)

The Welbike was manufactured in two versions: Mark I and Mark II (within the latter there were two series, differing between each other in minor modifications). The main difference between the versions was the mudguard over the rear

38 Driver's Handbook for Excelsior "Welbike"…, pp. 7-8.
39 *Maintenance Manual for Excelsior 98 cc. "Welbike"*, …, p. 2.

Nationality marking painted on the fuel tank and paratroopers of the 1st IPB during exercise with Welbike Mk I motorcycles (right) and War Department Number.

wheel added in the Mk II version. The motorcycles came in two paint schemes, characteristic for British military equipment. Usually motorcycles were painted in camouflage green, typically applied to all British vehicles. The other colour was brown, more often used on Welbike Mk IIs.

Polish paratroopers used Welbike Mk I motorcycles. It was intended to take a large number of them to the Operation Market Garden[40].

Motorcycles operated by the Polish parachute brigade wore unit markings. The distinguishing element was white oval with black PL (Poland) letters, the nationality marking. It was painted on both fuel tanks below the War Department Number, which was also painted on both tanks. This consisted of the letter C (motorcycle designation) and seven digits. It was painted in white[41]. The 1st IPB received a small batch of these motorcycles, probably of one of the two batches manufactured in 1942. In dedicated literature War Department Numbers of this batch from C4658444 to C5153413 are given[42]. However, photos of Polish Welbikes from the Polish Institute and Sikorski Museum's archive in London show that numbers painted on Polish motorcycles were different than the batch described above[43].

The motorcycle in modified form (with added lights and mudguards and changed shape of the fuel tanks) was popular even after the war, which is shown by the fact that it was produced for the civilian market until1954 as the "Corgi Scooter".

---

40 Analysis of documents regarding equipment lists of individual subunits of the 1st IPB ready to join combat in 1944 shows that the Brigade intended to use 82 Welbikes in the airborne assault operation. See: IPMS, sign. A.V.20/31/15 – doc. 5. However the Brigade dropped these motorcycles in favour of *Royal-Enfield WD/RE*.

41 Preserved examples in original livery had the number in dirty white, but it may be the effect of the paint fading after decades since the production date.

42 en.wikipedia.org/wiki/Welbike – access: 20.06.2015.

43 The number of the motorcycle operated by the 1st IPB in the foreground of featured archive photo from The Polish Institute and Sikorski Museum in London is probably C 1292361. See also featured color profile.

ROYAL ENFIELD WD/RE "FLYING FLEA" MOTORCYCLE

Soldiers of paratrooper units, particularly of battalions' and brigade services' headquarters, needed a means of transport even in the drop zone to properly supervise subunit gatherings and deliver orders to often dispersed subunits. In the first period after landing it was usually the only method to provide issue of proper orders.

In rough terrain the best in this role were motorcycles, usually light but powerful enough to hold their own. Such a motorcycle, with an engine of 125 cc displacement, was the Royal Enfield WD/RE, often called by the British the "flying flea".

This motorcycle was light enough to be carried by a single soldier and large wheels and quite powerful engine made it more useful than the Welbike folding motorcycle. Indeed, its advantages in combat, from Normandy to the end of the war, were praised by British soldiers, although not all... In the memorandum after Operation Market Garden the commander of Airborne Signals Company, Capt. Józef Burzawa, reported to the headquarters of the 1st IPB that the motorcycles proved to be of little use in his unit due to their vulnerability during air dropping, when the impact of the motorcycle in airdropping tubular crates against the ground caused damage to the motorcycle, often difficult to fix. The crates with motorcycles, belly-mounted under aircraft, often fell apart in flight prematurely, resulting in loss of the vehicle. Besides, the motorcycle was too heavy to be carried by military communications soldiers, heavily laden with their equipment[44].

The motorcycle weighed 126 lb (57 kg) and with tubular crate, in which it was jettisoned through the door[45] or carried beneath the fuselage, 200 lb (90.7 kg). The wheels, which in the original model bent on landing, were reinforced and the handlebar was adapted for folding before packing into the crate.

It was not a purely British design. The pattern for the "Flying Flea" was the German

Royal Enfield WD/RE125 cc lightweight motorcycle ready for use.

Royal Enfield WD/RE lightweight motorcycle in tubular crate with parachute. (EvT)

Specifications:
Gross weight: 65 kg
Engine displacement: 125 cc
Transmission: Three-speed, gear changing with a lever located on the right side of the fuel tank.
Maximum speed: 40 mph (64.4 km/h)

---

44   J. Burzawa, *Uwagi i spostrzeżenia z operacji "Market"*, IPMS, sign. A.V.20/31/40-doc.6, c. 6. Also Władysław Stasiak recollects the loss of Royal Enfield motorcycle in flight in his memoirs. See: W.K. Stasiak, *W locie szumią spadochrony, Wspomnienia żołnierza spod Arnhem*, Warsaw 1991, p. 137.

45   This method was quickly abandoned because the aircraft overflew the drop zone, often quite short, in several tens of seconds and jettisoning the motorcycle in cradle took too much time. Therefore the British airborne units preferred to transport the Royal Enfield WD/RE motorcycles to the battlefield aboard gliders or suspended like airdropping containers beneath the fuselage.

Soldiers of Airborne Signals Company loading Royal Enfield WD/RE into tubular crates before departure for Driel. (IPMS)

DKW RT 125, whose design of 1930 could not turn into full success due to the Jewish origin of the owners of the factory. When Hitler and his party came to power in Germany they had to leave Germany and established contact with the Royal Enfield factory. Even before the outbreak of the war a light motorcycle was developed on the basis of the German pattern, with 125 cc two-stroke engine. However, at that time there was no thinking about forming parachute units in Great Britain, thus a few successful examples that had been made served only as a sort of pattern. The RE factory started production of heavier military motorcycles, with 250 and 350 cc engines. The situation changed after several years, when the War Department started to seek a lightweight motorcycle for airborne units in 1942. In 1943 production of a motorcycle began, which had successfully undergone trials byf dropping by parachute in a special tubular crate, and was designated WD/RE[46].

ARIEL W/NG MOTORCYCLE

The Ariel W/NG was adapted for military use from the Ariel Red Hunter[47] racing motorcycle. It entered service in the British Army in 1940.

The military Ariel W/NG underwent several modifications required by wartime production. First, savings on metals required simplification of the manufacturing process, adopting the method of pressing instead of machining, as in the civil version. Mainly steel rather than light alloys was used. Due to shortage of natural rubber in later years the handlebar grips were padded with canvas, without using rubber[48].

The motorcycle had a larger clearance between the engine and the ground, which was related to its use in rough terrain. For these purposes the frame was modified so that the motorcycle was more rear wheel-heavy.

Shifting the centre of gravity gave more stability in the ride and allowed the rider to have a more upright position, hence less tiring. It resulted in good off-road handling characteristics.

Due to its popularity the Ariel was produced in several engine variants, both solo and with sidecar. The best for airborne forces was the version with 347 cc (350 OHV) four-stroke engine.

The military version of the Ariel was fitted with racks for equipment sacks (these were often infantry backpacks) on both sides of the rear wheel. To the rear mudguard a seat for passenger or baggage rack was mounted. Also specially profiled toolboxes were mounted on the rear wheel. The lights, as in all other vehicles, were fitted with special blackout hoods[49].

---

46 http://www.military-history.org/articles/back-to-the-drawing-board-the-royal-enfield-flying-flea.htm-access: 22.12.2015.
47 W. C. Haycraft, The book of the Ariel, London no year of issue, p. 3.
48 C. Orchard, S. Madden, British Forces motorcycles 1925-45, Sutton 2006, pp. 30-31.
49 *Ibidem*, p. 31.

Ariel W/NG 346 cc OHV solo of 1942. (http://www.yesterdays.nl)

The motorcycles were painted either plain olive green or English green. Black rubber pads mounted on both sides of the fuel tank were either removed or fell apart. They were certainly also removed to make room for the War Department Number. Hence in the archive photos the motorcycles are seen without these pads, only with the caption ARIEL[50].

These also may be converted civilian models, hence green boxes with white caption not painted over.

Due to its weight the motorcycle could only be carried to battle aboard a glider. In combat condition, like of other heavy motorcycles, it could be used immediately, just after landing and removal of securing chains, if only the landing did not end with a crash and damage to the freight carried aboard the glider.

On 19 September 1944 the Polish 1st Independent Parachute Brigade had 86 motorcycles in its inventory, probably all being Ariel 350 W/NG solo[51]. They were operated by virtually all subunits of the Brigade, particularly in light and an-

---

50   *Ibidem*, p. 31.

51   It resulted from an urgent memorandum of 24 June 1944 for the headquarters of the armed forces in Scotland in which all types

ti-tank artillery, communications and subunit headquarters for liaison duty[52]. However, due to reduced numbers of transport gliders provided by the British (only 35 instead of planned 100[53]), only 18 Ariel motorcycles were sent to combat on 18 and 19 September 1944[54].

Specifications:[1]
Manufacturer: Ariel
Model: W / NG
Engine displacement: 346 cc
Engine type: 4-stroke / OHV

Cylinders: 1
Weight: 169 kg
Bore/stroke: 72 x 85mm
Fuel tank capacity: 10 l
Maximum speed: 70 mph (112 km/h)

1   http://www.yesterdays.nl – access: 20.02.2016.

Left side view of Ariel W/NG 350 cc motorcycle engine compartment. (http://www.yesterdays.nl)

Right side view of Ariel W/NG 350 cc motorcycle engine compartment. (http://www.yesterdays.nl)

MATCHLESS G3L MOTORCYCLE

Analysis of archive documents, listing types of vehicles operated by the 1st IPB until entering combat in Operation Market Garden in September 1944[55] suggests that the Ariel 350 cc was the only type of heavy motorcycle[56] operated by the Brigade.

This situation changed in the post-battle period, particularly in later years, when the 1st IPB was deployed to occupied Germany. At that time the unit received many more heavy motorcycles, but the character of the unit's duty changed. Tasks of the Brigade included patrol and control duty, for which airborne motorcycles were not needed. The Ariel's role was successfully assumed by other types, used on a mass scale by infantry units. In case of the 1st IPB it was the Matchless G3L 350.

Archive photos from that period also show other motorcycles ridden by Polish paratroopers, but they probably were acquired by vehicle parks in a non-regulation way, hence only a note is made about them.

and numbers of vehicles in the inventory of the subunits of the 1st IPB at that time were listed. It reveals, that the only type of 350 cc motorcycle is Ariel – 97 examples. Obviously it cannot be excluded that from that time till the battle the Brigade could have received as replacements heavy motorcycles of other types. However, it is more probable that the type was not changed, only the number was limited during preparations for Operation Market Garden. See: Urgent memorandum. Subject: "B" Vehicles, IPMS, sign.: A.V.20/31/15 – doc. 23.

52   See Annex 2
53   J. Dyrda, *op. cit.*, p. 698.
54   P. Witkowski, *Polskie jednostki powietrznodesantowe na Zachodzie*, Warsaw 2009. pp. 392-403.
55   The list of vehicles in the inventory of the 1st IPB on 16 June 1944 – Annex 1.
56   In this case the term "heavy motorcycle" may be misleading, because the engine displacement of 350 cc does not justify using that term. But at that time the motorcycles of this engine displacement were in fact the heaviest of this type of vehicles operated by the 1st IPB, taking into consideration the actual purpose of the unit, i.e. airborne assaults.

Left: Motorcycle patrol of the 1st IPB Military Police on Matchless G3L 350 motorcycles. (P. Nowaczyk).
Right: Present-day photo of a Matchless in the livery of the 1st Airborne Division. (Z. Wojtczak)

Polish paratrooper with Matchless G3L 350 motorcycle. The motorcycle has a red tip to the front wheel mudguard, which was a wartime marking of a given subunit (battalion).

28

Above, left and right: Matchless G3L 350 motorcycles used by the 1st IPB during the occupation of Germany. In the photo on the right on the motorcycle is Cpl Antoni Szulakowski. (H. Szulakowska)

Below and right: Matchless G3L 350 motorcycle in post-war paint scheme, during occupation of Germany. (RN)

AUSTIN 10 HP (4X2)[57] LIGHT UTILITY

In 1944 the headquarters of every subunit of the 1st IPB, including the Brigade's HQ, had at their disposal light utility cars, combining features of passenger and cargo car. Usually these were Austin 10 HP Light Utility cars. According to the inventory of the Polish airborne unit's vehicles[58], its subunits operated 19, including five in the Brigade's HQ and Transport and Supply Company. Slightly fewer – three – were operated by the Airborne Signals Company. The remaining subunits had one vehicle at their disposal each.

This car fared well in garrison service, when travelling on roads, but featuring no all-wheel drive was unsuitable for offroad use. In fact it was a vehicle designed in 1939 by the Austin Motor Company Ltd. of Northfield, based on a chassis from the 1930s, intended for the civilian market.

The car featured a closed metal cab, seating the driver and passenger. Just aft of it was the pickup bed, consisting of a metal, canvas-clad framework. The cab had no rear wall, providing access to the cargo compartment. Just behind the seats of the driver and passenger two other seats were located in the cargo compartment, making the car a four-seat pickup. It was a vehicle suitable for troops in training in the garrison, rather unsuitable for real battlefield use, although it was used mercilessly, often as an ambulance, barely carrying one passenger on a stretcher.

The car was usually painted in typical British olive green and the upper part of the canvas cover was additionally painted in "Mickey Mouse" camouflage pattern. The War Department Number, preceded by the letter "M", was by regulation painted on the upper part of the door, beneath the window. On the right mudguard a white Parachutist Badge was painted and on the left one the subunit assignment badge. These markings were repeated on the vehicle's side.

Austin 10 HP Light Utility

---

57 4x2 – the digits specify number of wheels (in this case 4) and number of drive wheels (in this case 2).
58 *Urgent memorandum. Subject: "B" Vehicles…*

Specifications[1]:
Weights: empty 895 kg, gross weight 1,514 kg
Dimensions: 3.98 x 1.6 x 1.9 x 2.4 m, ground clearance 217 mm
Axle track: front 1.23 m, rear 1.3 m
Drive: 4x2
Powerplant: 4-cylinder liquid-cooled 1,237 cc G3-222AB inline engine, rated at 29.5 hp
Transmission: Four forward and one reverse gear
Maximum speed: on road 80 km/h
Fuel tank capacity: 39 litres
Range: on road 300 km
The car had the spare wheel and a shovel mounted on the cab top. The location certainly resulted from the need for easy access to these items in emergency situations and lack of room in the cargo compartment.

1   Maintenance manual and instruction book Car, 2-seater, 4×2, Austin Model G/YG. Light Utility 10 H.P, no place of issue, 1944, k. VI. http://www.dws-xip.pl/encyklopedia/vehutilaustin-uk/ – access: 6.07.2015

HILLMAN 10 HP 4X2 LIGHT UTILITY

Later, especially during the occupation of Germany, another light utility car resembling the Austin 10 HP in shape, the Hillman 10 HP, appeared in the Brigade. Its specifications and performance were comparable with the predecessor.

Hillman 10 HP (wikipedia)

Paratroopers of the 1ˢᵗ IPB pose with a Hillman 10 HP car (JD)

Specifications[1]:
Empty weight: 1,066 kg
Load capacity: 400 kg
Dimensions: 3.8 x 1.6 x 1.9 m, ground clearance 190 mm
Wheelbase: 2.362 m
Powerplant: 4-cylinder liquid-cooled 1,185 cc inline engine, rated at 30 hp/4,100 RPM
Transmission: Four forward and one reverse gear
Maximum speed: on road 80 km/h
Range: on road 300 km

1   http://www.dws-xip.pl/encyklopedia/vehutilhillman-uk/ – access: 14.02.2016.

WILLYS MB/ FORD GPW

Willys MB, or rather its lesser known derivative the Ford GPW, is a true legend, not only because it was exceptionally successful, beautiful and reliable design. This car became the world's pattern for a four-wheel drive off-road car. It went into history during the Second World War under the name Jeep.

Even today its common name cannot be fully explained, because its shrouded by myth, as is the design itself. It is said that the name Jeep was given after a helpful and very fast dog accompanying the protagonist of an American cartoon – Popeye the sailor. However, it was propagated by the test driver of Willys-Overland off-road car manufacturer, Irving "Red" Haussmann, who used the name Jeep several times in a press interview, presenting the company's new product. (Most probably a way of saying "GP", General Purpose!)

In July 1940 the US Department of Defence invited tender for design and production of light General Purpose four-wheel drive off-road car. The Army's interest was aroused by designs from Ford, Willys-Overland and Bantam. Willys won the tender and started production of the vehicle, designated MB, but this relatively small company could not cope with the Army's great demand for its product, hence in January 1942 the Ford company launched mass production of the standard Willys MB, designated Ford GPW[59], differing from the Willys MB in minor details. The most significant are shape of the front grille, which in the Ford was produced by flat bar welding (initial Ford GP version) and in the Willys the front plate was a single stamped element with grille slots (later versions of the Ford had a similar grille). Each factory stamped its own company names on the back on the left side, differences also included rating plates on the passen-

59   GPW – General Purpose Willys.

ger's side, with the manufacturer's logo, and number of openings in the front bumper[60] (two in the Ford). Both models also visually differ in the shape of the frame, in the Willys it is a transverse tube bent at both ends.

The Jeep was a lightweight, ¼ ton four-wheel drive vehicle. It proved to be very versatile design, becoming an artillery tractor, light armoured car and even heavy machine gun and rocket launcher platform. The Jeep had the advantage that when riding on the road it employed two-wheel drive via the rear axle drive, and when riding off-road the driver could additionally engage drive to the front axle, using the clutch. This action was very easy, as was the four-wheel drive ride hence the Jeep enjoyed great popularity among soldiers from the very beginning, also thanks to its design, simple and reliable in every climate.

For the airborne forces the Jeep was the perfect vehicle. Thanks to it light parachute infantry could take guns, towed by the Jeep, to the battlefield. The car was an outstanding means of transport for heavy equipment and weapons picked up in the drop zone. It quickly became a specialized vehicle, e.g. for military communications teams. Finally, it was the first vehicle which could drive on rough battlefields to evacuate wounded soldiers. Thanks to its small size, folding windshield and relatively light empty weight it could fit easily into a Horsa glider's cargo hold, even with a gun or two trailers. After landing the vehicle could immediately enter action without preparations.

From 1942 both companies (Willys and Ford) manufactured Jeeps slightly differing from each other. Until mid-1942 both companies stamped their logos, Willys and Ford, on the backs, but the necessity of attaching the petrol canisters in that place ended this practice. Also varying were rating plates with logos of both manufacturers and the number of openings in the front bumper (used in the technological process of stamping of this element).

The 1st IPB received Jeeps of both types relatively late, only a few weeks before the

Above: The first version Ford GP. Later versions (Ford GPW) were nearly identical to the Willys MB. At first glance there are differences in production of the front grille and height of the bonnet, which in the Ford, due to another type of engine, is lower than in the Willys. Note also the shape of the door.

Ford GPW in the markings of Airborne Anti-tank Artillery Squadron of the 1st IPB. (W. Zakrzewski / J. Kaleczyc)

battle. They came from the contract of February and March 1944, which is indicated by the War Department Numbers of vehicles operated by the Brigade[61].

Adaptation of the vehicles to service in an airborne unit, particularly those carried aboard gliders, was necessary, although the Poles made modifications not as extensive as the British.

The British often relocated blackout lights from the grille to the mudguards, because in the British Army they were also intended to mark the contour of the vehicle, hence the relocation to the outermost parts of the body. The Jeeps for

---

60   Probably these were technological openings for centreing of the element during stamping. They also served as openings venting the frame, which prevented corrosion, although this purpose seems to be rather accidental.

61   The contract for the British Army of February 1944 included vehicles with numbers from M5534138 through M5539649. See: J. Farley, *The Standardised War-Time Jeep 2 1941-1945*, no place of issue, 2009, p. 116.

British airborne forces also had the towing hook on the front, reinforced bumper and a triangular towing frame on the back.

The modifications were necessary to load the Jeep aboard the Horsa glider. The dimensions of the glider's cargo hold were only slightly larger than those of the vehicle, thus shortening of the bumpers, cutting out the right step, adaptation of the steering wheel[62], relocation of the spare wheel to the front or moving it so that it did not protrude beyond the contour of the body, was necessary.

This concerned the Horsa Mk 1, aboard which the Jeep was loaded via a loading ramp at the port cargo hold door, not the Mk 2, in which to open the cargo hold the nose with cockpit was hinged to the starboard side. During Operation Market Garden the 1st IPB used only Horsa Mk 1 gliders.

Below: Jeeps as artillery tractors and personnel carriers.

Above: Ford GPW, airborne version, of the Anti-tank Squadron of the 1st IPB. Method of carrying firearms in holders and small arms ammunition on the bonnet is visible. On the back of the vehicle a triangular towing frame, fitted in Great Britain, is visible. The Jeep has sawn-off front bumper with engineer's shovel and pickaxe.

Specifications[1]:
Gross weight: 1,476 kg
Load capacity: 400 kg
Dimensions: length 3.36 m, width: 1.57 m, height 1.75 m
Wheelbase: 2.03 m
Powerplant: 4-cylinder 4-stroke liquid-cooled 2,199 cc inline engine, rated at 60 hp
Maximum speed: on road 105 km/h, 50 km/h off-road
Range: 458 km

1   *Maintenance Manual for Willys Truck ¼ – Ton 4x4, Ohio 1942, s. 3; ¼ – Ton 4x4 Truck (Willys-Overland Model MB and Ford Model GPW)*, Washington 1944, pp. 10-12.

62   Adaptation of the steering wheel for glider transport initially consisted in cutting out its upper section, protruding beyond the car's contour, which converted it into a sort of yoke. Later the steering wheel was unscrewed. It was necessary because otherwise the Jeep could not move under the protruding wing spar, which made the Horsa's cargo hold lower.

British Jeeps on a ploughed field serving as artillery tractors. They were outstanding in this role, having virtually no rivals.
***Below:** Battery of 75 mm mountain howitzers towed to firing positions by Jeeps.*

Analysing the loadsheets of gliders (Annex 4) it can be noted that major modifications of the Jeeps made in the Brigade included hastily detached and easy to dismantle parts, such as windscreens, seats or spare wheels (see loadsheets of gliders Nos. 149 and 150 of the Airborne Medical Company).

It also seems that there was no time to apply camouflage patterns, as the British paratroopers did. The training in maintenance and operation of Jeeps in the Brigade had not been completed until entering action. Not driving, because

A Jeep of a military communications unit with R-19 wireless set installed on the left side.

The British patent for detachable steering wheel for glider transport.

Ford GPW, airborne version, of the Anti-tank Squadron of the 1st IPB. Method of carrying firearms in holders and small arms ammunition on the bonnet is visible. On the back of the vehicle a triangular towing frame, fitted in Great Britain, is visible. The Jeep has sawn-off front bumper with engineer's shovel and pickaxe.

Two Polish curiosities. Analysis of the upper photograph suggests that the War Department Number of the Jeep is not painted white, but light blue, as on the vehicles of the British 1st Airborne Division. Below, an atypical fully enclosed version of the Jeep used in the 1st IPB. Both photographs were taken during the occupation of Germany. (RN/ MS)

The parade of 1ˢᵗ IPB subunits on the occasion of receiving the unit's banner sent from the Homeland. The photo shows a Willys MB of 1942 Canadian contract, which is indicated by towing eyes on the bumper, left headlamp cover and early type of steering wheel.

A Jeep without (left) and with (right) War Department Number on the hood. (MS/RN)

this skill was quickly learned by the drivers. It concerns rather training in loading the Jeep into the Horsa Mk 1 glider. Even more difficult was unloading the vehicle, usually towing a trailer or cannon through the jettisoned tail section, when the combination of vehicles rode down metal ramps onto the ground.

Landing the glider was not easy and usually was accidental, in terrain such as a ploughed fields or meadows. The glider was usually bent, which additionally hampered unloading of vehicles via ramps taken for this purpose. Despite this, the powerful engine and rugged construction of the Jeep was invulnerable to these impediments.

Therefore Polish Jeeps remained in the original, single-colour factory paint scheme, with only unit insignia, bridge classification numbers and nationality markings added. There is a photograph published by George Cholewczyński in his

A Polish Jeep (the version adapted for glider transport) with 6-pounder gun during Operation Market Garden. (M. Szpara-gowski)

book "*Rozdarty naród*" ("The nation torn apart"), showing a Jeep of the Airborne Medical Company standing on airfield. The Jeep is complete, has canvas hood and and factory mounted grips. In lieu of the US star it has Red Cross markings painted on the bonnet (see picture).

The described vehicle sports also bridge classification numbers, unit and subunit insignia. The white star was painted on the left side, aft of the mudguard. It has no War Department Number[63].

It seems that this lack was quite common, because another archive photograph, taken during a parade on 15 June 1944, shows a Jeep without American stars and War Department Number (see below).

The right headlight was often covered by the bridge classification number plate and a hood constraining the light beam was mounted on the left one. In other cases the bridge classification number was painted under the windscreen. Things were a bit different during occupation of Germany, where the Jeeps admittedly still did not wear a camouflage pattern, but sported complete markings and featured even some modifications of the airborne Jeeps. Interestingly, not all had War Department Numbers painted on their hoods.

In contrast with the pre-battle period, in the archive photos from the occupation of Germany, the Brigade's Jeeps were increasingly more often made similar to vehicles of that type used by British airborne units.

Now it is difficult to determine whether this was caused only by the need of useful placement of the vehicle's assigned equipment. The desire to emphasize the unit's elitism, whose separate character and training was perhaps to be empha-sized by such details as the spare wheel mounted on the front grille or artillery round holders on the hood.

TRAILER, 10-CWT. LIGHTWEIGHT, GENERAL SERVICE FOR JEEP[64]

The trailers were used by nearly all units of the British Army equipped with the Jeeps. This car had a dedicated trailer with characteristic, curved sides. The British airborne forces simplified this design, making it also much lighter.

On the back the trailer had a towing eye to enable a Jeep to tow more than one trailer, as a kind of "road train". Typical tyre size for light trailers was 5.00" x 16", but 5.75" x 16" or 6.00" x 16" were also used.

The trailers were produced in three basic versions (in terms of the design, not the equipment carried). These were: No 1 Mk 1, No.2 and No. 2 Mk1. In the 1st IPB certainly the No.1 Mk.1 variant was used, which the list of equipment be-

Specifications[1]:
Total/box length: 278 cm/155 cm
Total/box width: 133 cm/89 cm
Total/box height: 107 cm/51 cm
Empty/maximum weight: 254 kg/760 kg

1 D. Fletcher, *Data Book of Wheeled Vehicles Army Transport 1939-1945*, edited by David Fletcher, London 1983, s. 703.

63 G. F. Cholewczyński, Rozdarty naród, Warsaw 2006, collection of archive photographs.
64 In military nomenclature these trailers were designated Trailer, 10-cwt. Lightweight lub Trailer ½ ton, cargo lightweight, 2-wheeled.
    See: R. van Meel, M. van Meel, British Airborne Jeeps 1942-1945. Modifications & Markings, Tilburg 2002, pp. 51, 56.

A Jeep (airborne version) of the British 1st Airborne Division with 10-cwt lightweight trailer for airborne units.

Lightweight trailer, in military nomenclature Trailer ½ ton, cargo, 2-wheeled, lightweight, No.1.

fore the battle (Annex 1), containing numbers of some trailers shows. The differences between versions consisted mainly in the design of the tow coupling and sides made of sheet metal, more rugged, with inner reinforcements (No.1), or made of wooden planks reinforced with metal angle bars (No.2).

No.1 Mk.1 versions were manufactured by Orme Evans Ltd, with numbers X4939020 – 4940455 and 5274487 – 5278086. The Brockhouse factory built one example, number X4940656. The SS Cars Ltd. factory manufactured trailers with numbers: X5278091 – 5281740 and X5845741 – 5845932. No1. Mk.2 trailers were manufactured by both Orme Evans and SS Cars Ltd. No. 2 versions were manufactured by Motor Panels Ltd. They had numbers: X6208181 – 6210180[65].

The trailers served also as platforms for various types of equipment:
- Versions manufactured by Royal Electric and Mechanical Engineers (REME):
- Electric generator – Power: 5 kW, 110 V DC for mechanical device,
- Electric lathe and drill,
- Electric generator for communications equipment,
- Electric repair set: grinder with polisher and drill,
- Water distillation set,
- 250 A welding machine with own generator and acetylene torch.
- Versions manufactured by Royal Engineers factory:
- Air compressor,
- 28" electric circular saw.

In 1943 REME designed also a special trailer with 100-gal water tank[66].

In the 1st IPB the trailers were mainly used as caissons for guns and howitzers and for carrying heavy equipment of individual subunits, such as the Airborne Engineer or Signals Companies. It seems that in both cases these were General

65 *Ibidem*, p. 51.
66 *Ibidem*, p. 51-52.

Service versions – a standard lightweight trailer with canvas hood. The latter was tied to the trailer with cords fastened to special hooks on the sides. The hoods were usually painted in "mickey mouse" camouflage pattern.

The Airborne Signals Company had a trailer with containers for communications equipment on the sides. This version was designated Trailer 2-wheeled Lightweight Stores. Its dimensions were different, total length: 282 cm, total width: 137 cm, total height: 118 cm, empty weight: 330 kg[67].

Trailer ½ ton, cargo, 2-wheeled, lightweight, No.1 (left) and No.2 (right). The trailers differ in the design of the towing hook, enabling attachment of another trailer. During operations on the Continent the canvas hoods were painted in camouflage patterns with an American star, a recognition marking for the Allied air forces.

A Jeep with another type of trailer – Trailer 10-cwt 2 WH. GS – with wooden plank sides reinforced with steel angle bars and load capacity in excess of 500 kg.

Another type of trailer with wooden box: Trailer, 1/2 ton, 2 wheeled, No.1.

67   , p. 704.

HUMBER FWD HEAVY UTILITY

A somewhat heavier car in this class was the Humber FWD HU. In the 1st IPB this vehicle was used as a staff car. The all-metal design of the body with six seats did not allow use of this vehicle on the battlefield e.g. for transport, hence it was used rather as Brigade's Headquarters representative car.

The 1st IPB probably received these cars in the post-battle period, which the archive photos show. On the list of Brigade's vehicles from 16 June 1944 these cars are not mentioned.

Above: Humber FWD HU in military green paint scheme, without camouflage, with War Department Numbers painted along the edges of the bonnet. The Parachutist Badge is painted on the right mudguard without the black box. Occupation of Germany.

Left: Humber FWD HU of the 1st IPB. Camouflage pattern and recognition markings painted on Allied vehicles during fighting on the Western Front in Europe. The Parachutist Badge is painted on the left mudguard. The photo was taken during inspection of the Brigade (1st Battalion) on 19 April 1945. (IPMS)

Specifications[1]:
Empty weight: 2,415 kg
Load capacity: 750 kg
Dimensions: 4.3 x 1.88 x 1.9 m, ground clearance 241 mm
Wheelbase: 2,8 m
Axle track: front 1.55 m, rear 1.54 m
Drive: 4x4
Powerplant: 6-cylinder liquid-cooled 4,086 cc inline engine, rated at 85 hp
Transmission: Four forward and one reverse gear, off-road reduction gear
Maximum speed: on road 100 km/h
Fuel consumption: 21 l/100 km

1   http://www.dws-xip.pl/encyklopedia/vehutilfwd-uk/ – access: 14.02.2016.

BEDFORD MWD 15-CWT[68]

The Bedford MWD 15-cwt (the full name is GS Bedford MWD Truck, 15-CWT 4x2) was one of the primary types of transport vehicles of this class in the 1st IPB. Prior to the battle the Brigade had 77, including eight of the 200 gal (909 l) water tanker version[69].

The truck had a cab with good visibility for the driver, thanks to the sloping bonnet. The vehicle was relatively low, which helped in camouflaging it. Aft of the cab was a wooden bed with rails for a canvas hood and benches for 10 infantrymen. This small truck could carry up to 800 kg of payload.

The Parachute Brigade used also the Bedfords in the drinking water tanker variant, the photo showing one such tanker sporting PL letters, of the 1st IPB transport column transported by sea during the operation of the Polish unit in the Netherlands in 1944. This version was designated Bedford MWC Water Tanker.

These tankers could also transport fuel, hence their mass use in RAF maintenance units. The tanker could be covered with tarpaulin stretched on steel rails, thanks to which it did not stand out among other trucks. Without this specific camouflage a fuel tanker could be a valuable target for the enemy air arm.

Vehicles of the 1st IPB transported by sea during Operation Market Garden. On the left the back of a Brigade's Bedford MWC Tanker is visible. (IPMS)

Truck 15-cwt 4x2 GS Bedford MWC Water Tanker, version operated by the 1st IPB. 900-l water tank mounted on Bedford chassis is visible. Note the method of mounting the spare wheel on the water tank.

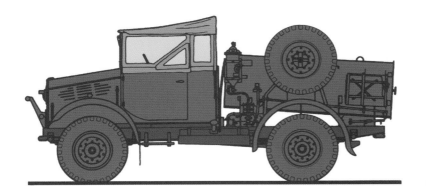
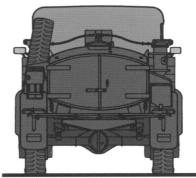

---

68   The symbol "cwt", e.g. 15-cwt – Imperial weight unit (hundredweight, 112 pounds), equal to ca. 50 kg. A 15-cwt truck has the load capacity of 750 kg, 30-cwt – 1,500 kg and 60-cwt – 3,000 kg.

69   *Urgent memorandum. Subject: "B" Vehicles…*

Bedford MWD 15-cwt trucks operated by the Military Police of the 1st IPB. The photo on the right shows the basic 750 kg truck variant, with wartime camouflage visible on the tarpaulin cover. On the left is a truck adapted for Military Police use. The method of post-war vehicle marking, with bumper tips painted white, is visible. Both photographs were taken during the occupation of Germany. (RN and below – IPMS)

Specifications[1]:
Empty weight: 2,100 kg
Load capacity: 10 infantrymen or 800 kg of cargo
Length: 4.38 m
Width: 1.99 m
Height: 1.93 m
Powerplant: 6-cylinder liquid-cooled 3,519 cc inline engine, rated at 72 hp
Maximum speed: 80 km/h

Bedford MWD 15-cwt truck of the 1st IPB, adapted for troop transport with Polish paratroopers in the foreground before a parade in Great Britain, 1944.

1   A. A. Kamiński, T. Szczerbicki, op. cit., pp. 368-369.

FORD/CHEVROLET "CANADA" CMP, 15 CWT (4X4)[70]

This was a medium truck, capable of carrying up to 750 kg of payload, although it was produced in many versions, such as water or petrol tanker, mobile repair workshop, command or communications vehicle[71].

For better off-road characteristics the truck had all-wheel drive. It was designed and built by Ford and Chevrolet in Canada during 1936-1940. It was manufactured during 1940-45.

In the 1st IPB it served as typical medium truck in many subunits. The truck had a standard bed with tarpaulin cover stretched on steel rails. On the top of the cab, over the passenger's seat, was a hatch for observation.

Although vehicles rolling out assembly lines of both factories (Ford and Chevrolet) were nearly identical, there were some differences between them, however. The main difference consisted in type of engine: the Ford was powered by 95 hp V8 engine and the Chevrolet was powered by 85 hp six-cylinder inline engine. As far as external details are concerned, the Ford had square-shaped eyes on the grille and the Chevrolet, rhombus-shaped[72].

Right: Chevrolet "Canada" CMP during stopover on the route of the 1st IPB troops' transit. Note smaller bridge classification number, which may indicate that the photograph was taken after the war. (P. Wybraniec)

Below: Chevrolet "Canada" used as a hearse during the funeral of a soldier of the 1st IPB. Occupation of Germany (JD)

---

70   The abbreviation stands for Canadian Military Pattern
71   http://www.bernardvanmeurs.nl/index.php?page=cmp-info-en – access: 15.07.2015.
72   *Ibidem.*

Above: Vehicle column of the 1st IPB during a stop-over. A Chevrolet "Canada" with a loudspeaker mounted on the cab top is visible in the foreground. (IPMS)

Left: Chevrolet "Canada" CMP, which is indicated by characteristic rhombus-shaped eyes of the grille, but there is no Chevrolet logo, however. (MS)

Specifications [1]:
Weight: 3,572 kg
Length: 5.18 m
Width: 2.13 m
Height: 2.95 m
Powerplant: Chevrolet: 6-cylinder liquid-cooled Chevrolet GM 216 inline engine, rated at 85 hp; Ford: Ford 239 V8 engine, rated at 95 hp.
Maximum speed: 80 km/h

1 https://360carmuseum.com/en/museum/38/exhibit/2038 – access: 14.07.2015.

FORD/FORDSON WOT2 GS

Ford Fordson WOT[73] was a series of cars made during the Second World War in the Ford factory near London. The name Fordson originated from the combination Henry Ford & Son.

It was one of the first car types introduced to the British Army to motorize it in the early 1930s. Fordson WOT2 4x2 quickly became the standard truck of 750 kg payload capacity, and heavier versions (to WOT 6) complemented the remaining needs of British transport units.

It was a popular and widely used design, which could serve in its standard form, in which the payload was transported on a traditional truck bed, protected against weather by a tarpaulin cover stretched on rails. The truck was produced in several versions, also serving as platforms for Polsten and Hispano-Suiza anti-aircraft cannons. Versions produced from 1943 had a larger windscreen, which allowed fitting of a canvas hood, better protecting against rain. This truck was produced during 1939-1945 by the Ford Motor Company Ltd of Dagenham and used even after the war, until the early 1950s, when it was replaced by 1-ton trucks[74].

The Polish Parachute Brigade also used the Fordsons as artillery tractors for 75 mm mountain howitzers, with which the Airborne Light Artillery Squadron was armed. To adapt the vehicle for the needs of the airborne forces, it was stripped of unnecessary elements, such as the tarpaulin cover and rails. The originally designed open cab, also with canvas hood, was also dismantled and the driver and despatcher were protected against the wind only by small separate windscreens. The doors were made of canvas sheets. The bed was equipped with benches for the gun crew in two rows facing each other. This configuration was sufficient for the crew with the gun.

Later version of Fordson WOT 2, with larger windscreen and metal doors. This a typical 750 kg (15-cwt) truck.

Specifications[1]:	Powerplant: V8 liquid-cooled 3,621 cc engine, 60
Weight: 3,327 kg	hp/2,840 RPM
Length: 4.50 m	Transmission: 4-speed
Width: 2.00 m	Electric system: 12 V (early models 6 V)
Height: 2.28 m	Brakes: Mechanical
	Fuel: Petrol
1 *Ibidem.*	Fuel tank capacity: 104 l

73   WOT stands for: War Office Trucks.
74   http://www.armyvehicles.dk/fordwot2.htm – access: 20.08.2015.

Fordson WOT 2 artillery tractor during a parade in front of the President of the Republic of Poland in exile, Władysław Raczkiewicz, and Commander-in-Chief Gen. Kazimierz Sosnkowski in 1944. (IPMS)

MORRIS-COMMERCIAL C8/AT

This vehicle was designed as tractor for 2-pounder anti-tank guns, which could be transported on the platform behind driver's compartment, unloaded and placed on other firing position when needed. As a traditional artillery tractor the C8 had an open cab, which however could be covered by a canvas hood stretched on rails, but had no windscreen or cab top support. The driver's compartment consisted basically of a row of seats, on which, apart from the driver, 2-3 soldiers of the anti-tank or other gun crew could sit. Two metal sheets with holders for small items of equipment protected the seat occupants[75].

Left: Morris-Commercial C8/AT as artillery tractor. The truck has no tarpaulin cover and the platform behind the cab, originally intended for carrying a 2-pdr gun, is used for transporting the gun crew. (MS)
Right: Morris-Commercial C8/AT towing a 6-pounder gun. The bed is covered with tarpaulin. (IPMS)

75 http://www.wheelsofvictory.com/Morris%20commercial%20c8%20P.html – access: 25.12.2015.

The rails could be attached to the platform, which allowed for quick construction of a tarpaulin-covered truck bed, on which other soldiers of the gun crew could seek cover against the rain.

The Brigade's tractors were also used with 6-pounder guns or American 75 mm howitzers. These artillery pieces were always towed, because carrying them on the platform was impossible and impractical. After the withdrawal of the 2-pdr gun from the equipment of the platform the tractor received the military designation Truck 4x4 C8/AT (anti-tank)[76].

The trucks were equipped with steel rails for unloading guns from the platform, but it was a reminder of its original use with the 2-pdr gun, which due to rapid development of German armour became useless. So, they often were redundant ballast. In fact this truck was a mean of transport for the gun and its crew of eight.

Morris-Commercial C8/AT artillery tractor. The seating of the gun crew is visible. (MWP)

Specifications[1]:
Weight: 4,027 kg
Length: 4.57 m
Width: 2.08 m
Height: 2.16 m
Powerplant: 4-cylinder liquid-cooled 3,519 cc inline engine rated at 70 hp.
Transmission: 5-speed
Electric system: 12 V
Brakes: Hydraulic
Fuel: Petrol
Fuel tank capacity: 2x 50 l
Maximum speed: 80 km/h
Range: 384 km (240 miles)

1   A. A. Kamiński, T. Szczerbicki, op. cit., pp. 383-383

MORRIS C8 QUAD (FAT) ARTILLERY TRACTOR

The vehicle was designed in 1938 for the 25-pounder gun. This distinctive fully enclosed vehicle was intended to tow the gun and carry its crew and ammunition supply. They were produced in three versions (Mk I – III), differing from each other in details, mainly in the possibility of disengaging the front axle drive.

To make the tractor similar to an ordinary truck, the sloping rear of the bed was covered by a canvas hood on rails, which made the vehicle similar to the cargo version and did not attract enemy attention. The 1st IPB also operated these tractors, which the archive photos show[77].

Morris C8 FAT of the 1st IPB towing a 6-pounder gun on a parade. (MWP)

76   *Ibidem.*
77   M. Skotnicki, *1.Samodzielna Brygada Spadochronowa 1942-43*, "Poligon" Issue 2, 2008, p. 80.

Morris C8 FAT artillery tractor with a gun and limber crossing a river. (IWM H20971)

Specifications[1]:
Weight: 3,402 kg
Length: 4.49 m
Width: 2.21 m
Height: 2.26 m
Powerplant: 4-cylinder liquid-cooled 3,519 cc Morris EH inline engine rated at 70 hp.
Electric system: 12 V
Fuel: Petrol
Maximum speed: 68 km/h
Range: 385 km

1   A. Zasieczny, *Broń Wojska Polskiego 1939-1945...*, p. 97; A. A. Kamiński, T. Szczerbicki, *op. cit.*, pp. 382-383.

AUSTIN K2/Y AMBULANCE

The only cars belonging to the 1st Independent Parachute Brigade which, apart from the Jeeps, took part in the battle fought by Polish paratroopers for Driel were the Brigade's ambulances, which on 24 September managed to make their way to Driel, defended under siege to evacuate Polish soldiers heavily wounded during the previous days. These cars were Austin K2/Y (Ambulance) of the Airborne Medical Company. The ambulances delivered dressings and other medical supplies, including blood plasma, necessary for transfusions to the field hospital, located in the school in Driel. Thanks to the sacrifice of the am-

Polish Austin K2/Y ambulances of the Airborne Medical Company at the field hospital in Driel on the morning of 24 September. Later the hospital was hit several times by German mortar shells. (J.Moździerz/GZ)

Ambulances of the 1ˢᵗ IPB Airborne Medical Company. The photo was taken in the post-battle period, probably during the occupation of Germany. (RN)

bulance crews, which reached the positions of their units via the only available road, often crossed by the Germans, 77 heavily wounded were evacuated to hospitals in Nijmegen[78].

They departed for the Operation "Market Garden" within the first naval component of the Brigade, which steamed off for the Continent on 15 August[79] 1944 and reached the Brigade within the ground forces participating in the operation.

Specifications:
Empty weight: 3 tonnes 1 ½ cwt (3,124 kg)
Length: 5.49 m
Width: 2.26 m
Height: 2.79 m
Crew: 2-3 (driver and paramedics)
Powerplant: 6-cylinder liquid-cooled 3,462 cc Austin inline engine rated at 60 hp.
Transmission: 4-speed
Fuel tank capacity: 2x 54.5 l
Maximum speed: 80 km/h
Inner dimensions of the rear body are 2.6 x 2.0 m and height 1.7 m. The casualties compartment was accessible through double rear doors or smaller front doors from the cab[1].

1   L.B. Kašeev, Britanskie vojennye mašiny 1939-1945, no place and year of issue, pp. 14-15.

78   J. Golba, Służba zdrowia w działaniach 1.Sam. Bryg. Spad. Pod Arnhem-Driel, IPMS, sign: A.V.20/31/43-doc.14, c.54.

79   On that day, 15 August 1944 columns of vehicles were formed, heading for the Continent under Operation Transfigure – the first variant of use of British and Polish airborne units in France in the area of Rambouillet and Saint-Arnoult-en-Yvelines. The progress of friendly ground forces soon made it no longer needed, but the machine of use Allied airborne forces was not stopped, hence the series of evolutions of the plan "Transfigure" into repeatedly new forms and operations on increasingly larger scale, until the eventual plan, i.e. the "Market Garden" of 17 September 1944. Despite the changes of the plan the naval component reached Normandy beaches and the naval component of the 1ˢᵗ IPB landed on "Juno" beach on 19 August. See: A. Tokarz, Historia I. rzutu morskiego I.Sam. Brygady Spadochronowej, IPMS, sign. A.V.20/31/46-doc.13, c.1 (in this document wrong date of the landing in Normandy, 18 August was given); A. Tokarz, (Meldunek dowódcy 1.SBS z dn. 16.10.1944 r.), IPMS, sign: A.V.20/32/46-doc. 12, c.52.

Within the first naval component seven ambulances were transported. One of them was destroyed in a road accident in Cambridge on 15 August[80]. During the operation itself ambulances without further losses continued their mission, bringing back to England the remaining six vehicles[81].

This version of special duty military vehicle was based on the civilian Austin K30 truck. However, in the military version the doors were replaced by canvas sheets. The ambulance could carry ten sitting or four lying casualties. The rear body, (No. 2 Mk I/L) was developed by the Royal Army Medical Corps and built by the Mann Egerton company.

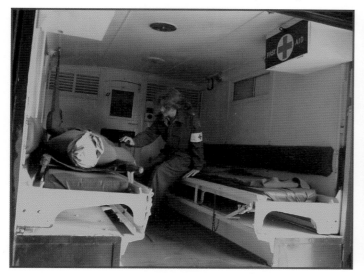 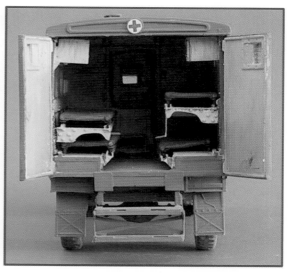

Interior of Austin K2 ambulance. It could be reconfigured to carry more casualties on stretchers. (Robin Buckland)

 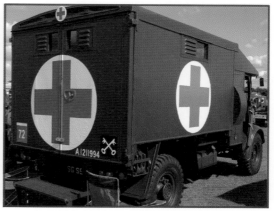

Austin K2 ambulance wearing insignia of a British unit, with different standard markings. A single cross is painted on the back, as in archive photos of Polish ambulances at Driel. There was also a version with two crosses, one on each door. (Robin Buckland)

BEDFORD OYD LORRY GS

Initially this car was designed for the civilian market, but the war forced development of a military version. The commercial "OL" version was simplified and adapted

A column of trucks. Bedfords OYD GS of the Transport and Supply Company of the 1st IPB (first naval component) are visible in the background. Preparations for embarkation for return to England, October 1944. (IPMS)

80 A. Tokarz, Historia I. rzutu morskiego..., c.1.

81 Wykaz pojazdów mechanicznych I rzutu morskiego w drodze na kontynent i w drodze powrotnej, IPMS, sign. A.V.20/31/46-doc.12 C i D, c. 63-64 (Annex 3).

for unsophisticated, but hard, transport duty. The new series of vehicles delivered to the British Army was designated "OY". The version "OYD" was a general purpose truck with bed covered by tarpaulin stretched on steel rails. In the 1st IPB the version with an extended bed (lorry) was also used.

Bedford OYD GS. (IWM H14423)

Specifications[1]:
Empty weight: 2,697 kg
Length: 6.22 m
Width: 2.18 m
Height: 3.09 m
Powerplant: 6-cylinder liquid-cooled 3,519 cc inline engine rated at 72 hp.
Electric system: 12 V
Load capacity: 1.5 – 3 tonnes
Range: 450 km
Maximum speed: 65 km/h

1   A. A. Kamiński, T. Szczerbicki, op. cit., pp. 372-373; http://www.armyvehicles.dk/bdoy.htm – access: 13.07.2015;

FORD/FORDSON WOT3 30-CWT, 4×2, GS

This car was a lightweight version of a truck. In the Brigade it was used as artillery tractor, serving also for transport of the gun crew. The truck had a bed with wooden sides and steel, downwards-opening tailgate. Benches for soldiers, accommodating up to 8-10 paratroopers with basic equipment, were mounted along the sides. The truck bed could be covered by a tarpaulin stretched on steel rails.

The trucks were painted all green. On the tailgate (or the bar below, if the tailgate was removed) the War Department Number and white oval with black PL letters were painted. On the toolbox on the left side the white Parachutist Badge/Brigade's emblem was painted. Initially it was stencilled on a black background with white outline, but later, to save time, the emblem was painted directly on the body,

Fordson WOT3 Lorry bearing War Department Number L1289479 transporting a parachute rifle squad with equipment during a parade in 1944. (IPMS)

as on other vehicles in the late war and post-war period. Additionally a white War Department Number was painted on both cab doors. Moreover, on the right mudguard (looking from the front) the Parachutist Badge was painted. The number indicating assignment to a given subunit was added on the left front mudguard as well as a yellow disc with bridge classification number.

Fordson WOT3 Lorry bearing War Department Number L1289431 of Airborne Light Artillery Squadron, towing a 75 mm howitzer with crew in 1944. (IPMS)

Specifications[1]:
Empty weight: 2,940 kg
Length: 5.8 m
Width: 2.2 m
Height: 2.6 m
Powerplant: 8-cylinder liquid-cooled 3,622 cc inline engine rated at 85 hp.
Load capacity: 1,500 kg
Maximum speed: 60 km/h

1   http://www.dws-xip.pl/encyklopedia/sam-wot3/ – access: 12.07.2015.

Above left and right: Fordson WOT3 as artillery tractor – version with shorter bed, adapted for troop transport. Open cab could be protected by a canvas hood, the windscreen could be removed. Below – the rear view. Both vehicles belong to various subunits, but the markings show, that they were only borrowed as artillery tractors. (MWP)

DODGE T-110/D-60 L (4X2)

Dodge D-60 trucks delivered to the British Army from 1940 were products of the Canadian subsidiary of the Dodge company. These trucks of T-110 series were powered by six-cylinder 95 hp engines. They were most popular in Europe. There were two basic models: T110L (D-60S) and T110L-9 (D-60L).

The models differed from each other in axle track – the S version had a track of 3,454 mm and the L version 4,064 mm[82]. These versions were fitted with wheels of larger diameter than those of the civilian model. The truck had a conventional bed, which could be covered by a tarpaulin stretched on rails. It could carry a 3-tonne payload.

Dodge T-110 of the 1st IPB, occupation of Germany. (Wilkowski family archive)

Specifications[1]:
Empty weight: 2,928 kg
Length: 6.65 m
Width: 2.28 m
Height: 3.17 m
Powerplant: 6-cylinder liquid-cooled 3,878 cc inline engine rated at 95 hp.
Electric system: 12 V
Load capacity: 3.4 tonnes (versions with longer bed – 4.5-5 t)

---

1   A. A. Kamiński, T. Szczerbicki, *op. cit.*, pp. 376-377.

LEYLAND RETRIEVER (TRUCK 6X4 3-TON)

This vehicle was one of the largest trucks the Brigade operated. It was in use probably only in the pre-battle period. The only example was operated by the Transport and Supply Company. Probably the 1st IPB operated a Leyland of older version, with open cab. The numbers of the vehicle on the list allow assumptions that it was the B version – mobile repair workshop with milling machine and column drilling machine[83].

Indeed at that time, the due to its character and size the Polish unit did not need more such large trucks. The situation changed when after the battle of Arnhem the last reorganization of the unit took place. Then the demand for such means of transport increased and this obsolete and

Leyland Retriever 6x4, 3-ton – older version, with open cab. (IWM H8164)

---

82   http://www.maquetland.com/article-phototheque/5726-dodge-t-110-l-9 – access: 19.02.2016.
83   Urgent memorandum. Subject: "B" Vehicles, IPMS, sign. A.V.20/31/15 – doc. 23, Annex 1.

primitive design was replaced by modern American trucks, such as Studebakers.

The Leyland Retriever was a 6x4 truck manufactured by Leyland Motors during 1939-1945. The design was characterized by English-style simplicity. The older version, used by the 1st IPB, had an open cab without windscreens. When raining, only a primitive canvas hood could be stretched on rails and the driver and passenger could put on special aprons protecting against the rain and cold[84]. The later variant had a metal cab with windscreens, but as in the older model, there was no door, only a canvas sheet – typical for British trucks[85].

The design was based on a three-axle chassis with powered rear axles. The fuel tank capacity was 141 l. The spare wheel was mounted between cab and bed. There were numerous versions of this vehicle, from ordinary trucks to several specialized technical vehicles, such as crane, mobile repair workshop, searchlight platform or gantry.

Specifications[1]:
Length: 6.85 m
Width: 2.27 m
Height: 3.45 m
Powerplant: 4-cylinder liquid-cooled Leyland 5,895 cc inline engine rated at 73 hp.
Transmission: 4-speed
Brakes: hydraulic with servo assistance
Fuel: petrol
Tank capacity: 141 l
Range: 312 km

1   British Army Transport 1939-45. Tank Transporters, Recovery Vehicles, Machinery Trucks, red. M.P. Conniford, vol.1, Micham Surrey, 1972, p. 8; http://www.armyvehicles.dk/leylandretriever.htm – access: 29.12.2015;

AUSTIN K5 GS (4X4)

The Austin K5 was a heavy truck produced by this company. It could carry a payload of up to 3 tonnes. Its basic version, GS (General Service), was a conventional design with wooden truck bed behind the cab, which could be covered by a tarpaulin stretched on rails.

Two Austin K5s of the 1st IPB during a stopover. One has a Red Cross sign painted on the top, which may suggest that it was assigned to the Airborne Medical Company. Note the distinctive "mickey mouse" camouflage applied on the tarpaulin covers and upper surfaces. (IPMS)

84   http://www.nationaltransportmuseum.org/mv001.html – access: 29.12.2015.
85   http://www.armyvehicles.dk/leylandretriever.htm – access: 29.12.2015

Austin K5 3-ton truck of the 1st IPB during occupation of Germany. (P.Wybraniec)

Alfhausen, Germany, 1946, PFC Grzegorz Stanowski of the 1st IPB standing next to an Austin K5 truck. (MIT)

Specifications:
Empty weight: 3,740 kg
Gross weight: 7.355 kg
Length: 5.99 m
Width: 2.28 m
Height: 3.0 m
Axle track: 1.8 m
Wheelbase: 3.66 m
Powerplant: 6-cylinder liquid-cooled Austin 3,995 cc inline engine rated at 82 hp.
Transmission: Four forward and one reverse gear, off-road reduction gear
Fuel tank capacity: 145 l
Range: 430 km
Maximum speed: 62 km/h

FORD/FORDSON WOT 6

During the last reorganization of the 1st IPB, after the unit's return from Operation Market Garden, several changes were introduced. The attempt to re-form and expand the unit was being done in conjunction with changes of some means of transport. This is apparent in archive photos, in which new (other) types of trucks than during the pre-battle period appear. One of them is the Fordson WOT 6, a 3-ton 4x4 truck, powered by a Ford V8 petrol engine[86]. It was usually built with conventional tarpaulin-covered bed (GS version), or as specialized technical vehicles.

Ford/Fordson WOT6 4x4 truck of the 1st IPB during occupation of Germany. (J.D.)

---

86   British Army Transport 1939-45…, p. 7.

Specifications[1]:
Empty weight: 3,930 kg
Length: 6.22 m
Width: 2.18 m
Height: 3.09 m
Powerplant: 6-cylinder liquid-cooled 3,519 cc inline engine rated at 72 hp.
Electric system: 12 V
Load capacity: 1.5 – 3 tonnes
Range: 450 km
Maximum speed: 65 km/h

1   http://www.armyvehicles.dk/fordwot6.htm – access: 29.12.2015; British Army Transport 1939-45..., p. 7.

STUDEBAKER US 6

The Studebaker US 6 was a 6x6 or 6x4 off-road military truck with 2.5 tonne load capacity. It was one of the legendary trucks of the Second World War, a true "workhorse" of Allied armies. During 1941-1945 approximately 200,000 were produced. While externally very similar GMC CCKW 352 and 353 trucks were delivered to the US Army, the Studebaker US6 entered production to fulfil the Lend-Lease Act demands and the Soviet Union became the main recipient (ca. 100,000)[87].

It was a design very much appreciated by the soldiers due to

A Studebaker US 6 of the 1st IPB, carrying 16 parachute riflemen with light armament during a parade. (MWP)

Studebaker US 6, cargo version for personnel and materiel transport. (wikipedia)

87   A. Zasieczny, op. cit., p. 147.

extreme ruggedness, even when operated in very hard conditions, and easy to repair. It was superior to English trucks, especially in its capabilities and load capacity (2,500 kg). The Studebaker US6 could climb slopes up to 30° loaded, which often eliminated the British rivals.

The truck was produced in 13 versions (U1 through U13), which is a proof of its reliability and versatility. The versions differed in purpose (general service truck, tanker, semi-tractor) and technical features, such as wheelbase, type of drive-train or winch. As a troop carrier the US6 transported 16 infantrymen with equipment, sitting on benches along the sides and three in the cab. The bed could be covered with a tarpaulin stretched on rails[88].

Specifications[1]:
Weight: depending on the version – from 3,715 kg (6x4 tractor) to 13,607 kg (6x4 tractor with semi-trailer).
Cargo version: ca. 4,500 kg
Load capacity: 2.5 – 5 tonnes
Length: 6.36 m (6.73 m with winch)
Width: 2.23 m
Height: 2.24 m
Powerplant: 6-cylinder liquid-cooled Hercules JXD 5,240 cc inline engine rated at 95 hp.
Electric system: 6 V
Main brakes: drum type on all wheels with servo assistance
Fuel: petrol
Fuel tank capacity: 150 l
Range: 390 km
Maximum speed: 70 km/h

1   2 ½-ton 6x6 truck and 2 ½-ton to 5-ton 6x4 truck (Studebaker models US6 and US6x4), Washington 1943, pp. 5-16.

UNIVERSAL CARRIER

This was a light armoured carrier, serving as a platform for infantry support or anti-tank weapons, such as the Boys rifle, Bren light machine gun, Vickers heavy machine gun or 50.8 mm mortar. It was also used as a tractor for the 6-pounder gun, scout, command or liaison vehicle.

The 1st IPB operated these vehicles. Analysis of photographs by the author suggests that the largest number of Carriers were used during the occupation of Germany, which photos from parades, in which several of these vehicles took part, show. However, more interesting is the fact that a Carrier (probably a single example) was operated by the Polish parachute unit circa 1943, when its crew wear paratrooper uniforms, but without the Denison smocks, which indicates the time the photograph was taken.

Soldiers of the 1st IPB parade in a Universal Carrier in front of Gen. Marian Kukiel. Scotland, late 1942 or early 1943. (IPMS)

88   2 ½-ton 6x6 truck and 2 ½-ton to 5-ton 6x4 truck (Studebaker models US6 and US6x4), Washington 1943, pp. 5-16.

Soldiers of the 1st IPB riding a Universal Carrier. A para-chute painted on the right side is visible. Scotland, 1942 or early 1943. (IPMS)

A restored Universal Carrier (early model) with characteristic side mudguards.

Universal Carriers in a parade of 1st IPB subunits during the occupation of Germany. Lack of additional side mudguards is visible. (RN)

Specifications[1]:
Traction: tracks
Gross weight: 3,700 kg
Crew: 2-5 (depending on version and purpose)
Length: 3.7 m
Width: 1.94 m
Height: 1.57 m
Ground clearance: 220 mm
Powerplant: 8-cylinder liquid-cooled Ford GAE/GAEA engine rated at 65 hp.
Range: 180 km (on road) 120 km (off-road)
Maximum speed: 48 km/h (on road)

1   http://www.army1914-1945.pl/polska/wojska-ladowe-ii-rp/uzbrojenie-wyposazenie-i-sprzet-wojsk-ladowych-ii-rp/pojazdy-bojowe-ii-rp/279-universal-carrier-mk-i-w-psz-na-zachodzie-technika – access: 15.07.2015.

FIELD CANTEENS OF THE 1ST IPB

The 1st IPB also sent two field canteens to Operation Market Garden. They departed within the first naval component, as a part of the Brigade's headquarters[89]. The canteens served food, drinks and cigarettes – a necessary luxury to a soldier, often being the only currency in trenches.

The canteens were a vital factor for keeping troop morale high. Their arrival allowed the soldiers, often psychologically or physically harmed in combat, to forget bad memories for a moment. There are numerous accounts of the veterans, who reminisce the arrival of field canteens in the vicinity of the battlefield or troop quarters and link them with the improvement of soldiers' moods.

The analysis of archive photos preserved at The Polish Institute and Sikorski Museum in London allows us to specify types of vehicles serving as mobile canteens in the 1st IPB, at least those used in the Arnhem operation.

The first mobile field canteen that can be find in the London iconographic material is based on Austin passenger car, but the author was not able to specify the version exactly as the available photograph shows it only from the front, but the car's design corresponds with Austin versions from the early 1930s. Another canteen, whose photograph has been preserved in better condition, was built on Ford Eifel platform. The photograph of this canteen is available in the book of Andrzej A. Kamiński, *Od "Acromy" do "Zwycięzcy"*[90].

A field canteen based on an Austin passenger car of unspecified type (probably Austin Open Road Tourer) during the Brigade's disembarkation after the return from Operation Market Garden at the port of Tilbury on Thames in England on 12 October 1944. (IPMS)

Officers of the 1st IPB during operation Market Garden standing next to a camouflaged field canteen. Probably it is the vehicle based on an Austin car described above, which the spoked wheels show. Second from left is Capt. Ludwik Zwolański and second from right is 1st Lt Alfons Pronobis. (IPMS)

---

89   Wykaz pojazdów mechanicznych I rzutu morskiego w drodze na kontynent i w drodze powrotnej, IPMS, sign: A.V.20/31/46-doc.12 C, c. 63.

90   A. A. Kamiński, Od "Acromy" do "Zwycięzcy", vol. 10, Kraków, no year of issue, p. 389, lower left picture.

Polish and British paratroopers at a field canteen of unspecified type, probably Polish, which the Brigade's tabs on the collar of the woman serving the soldiers show. Operation Market Garden. (IPMS)

GLIDERS AND AIRCRAFT

AIRSPEED AS.51 HORSA

For the Polish parachute brigade, which had no heavy artillery or armoured vehicles, the most useful glider was the Horsa medium glider, which was used in the operation at Arnhem.

The Airspeed Aviation Company Ltd Horsa could carry, apart from two pilots, either 28 soldiers, two Willys Jeep cars or the set of a Jeep with a gun, ammunition supply and skeleton crew, depending on the load variant. Modifications of the equipment carried were possible within the maximum load capacity of 3,797 kg[91].

There were two variants of this glider, but the 1st IPB used only the earlier AS.51 Horsa Mk I variant. It was poorer version without hinged nose, which facilitated loading very much (applied in the Horsa Mk II).

Cargo loading in the Mk I version was accomplished through a cargo door on the port side, located just aft of the cockpit. The biggest problem was with loading a Jeep, because it was largest of all the equipment that could be transported by the glider. Therefore the pilots and crew of the vehicle transported had to combine efforts in executing several difficult manoeuvres to turn the vehicle and place it aboard the glider properly. To avoid repeating these arduous actions in the landing zone, when every second was very important, the cargo was unloaded through the rear opening after jettisoning the tail section.

This was accomplished by detonation of factory mounted explosives in the tail section[92]. This system was often unreliable, especially after a not perfectly clean landing, so the wooden tail section, which could not be separated mechanically, was simply chopped off with axes. It made the unloading faster, but caused destruction of the glider[93].

After the separation of the tail section the vehicles and other cargo were unloaded on purposely carried ramps.

Much better was the Mk II variant with nose with cockpit hinging to starboard, which enabled driving in and out of the cargo hold[94].

---

91 T. Królikiewicz, Encyklopedia szybowców wojskowych, Warsaw 1999, p. 42.

92 *Ibidem*, p. 43

93 Therefore before the invasion of Normandy a system of eight bolts, allowing for hinging or separation of the tail section, was used. This system often failed on hard landing, which damaged the structure of the airframe. In such a case again most efficient was chopping off the tail section with the axe.

94 T. Królikiewicz, *op. cit.*, p. 44.

A Horsa glider in flight, towed by an aircraft. The camou-flage pattern is visible on the upper surfaces, the sides and bottom are black. The photo was taken during a flight prior to the invasion of the Continent (note lack of invasion stripes). (IWM CH 10891)

The glider was towed by a heavy bomber. After having reached the landing zone area, the glider pilot disengaged from the towplane and glided to land on his own.

A very important skill was proper placement and securing of the load before take-off, to prevent it from moving in flight, which destabilised the glider. Much depended on the skills of the pilots, who had to be able to land a 7-ton wooden glider usually in uncertain, often rough terrain. To make it easier, each item of equipment and weapon had a specific weight in pounds. Each soldier knew his weight and being equipped with standard (weighed) equipment and weapon, could say his weight equipped and armed.

Knowing this data, the loadmaster could use a special device, a model of the glider's fuselage, being also scales to define the location of the glider's centre of gravity and maximum load using weights. It prevented an in-flight crash caused by relocation of the centre of gravity.

Since 1943, when the 1st Parachute Brigade received its independent status and the unit's core had been formed, consideration of adaptating gliders for carrying artillery pieces and heavy equipment to the battlefield began. At the same time the problem of acquiring or training their own glider pilots, who after landing did not complete their task but jined in combat, appeared.

The Brigade, still struggling with replacements, was not able to detach a large number of selected soldiers to train them as glider pilots in British units and schools[95].

General Sosabowski's arguments, included in the answer for a letter from Commander-in-Chief's headquarters on 30 June 1944:

The axe belonging to the Horsa's onboard equipment, used for chopping off the tail section in case of explosive failure.

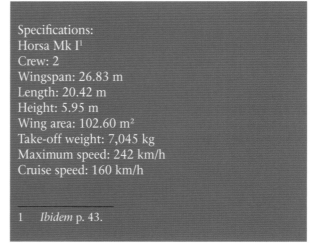

Specifications:
Horsa Mk I[1]
Crew: 2
Wingspan: 26.83 m
Length: 20.42 m
Height: 5.95 m
Wing area: 102.60 m²
Take-off weight: 7,045 kg
Maximum speed: 242 km/h
Cruise speed: 160 km/h

---

1   *Ibidem* p. 43.

---

95   The estimations of Gen. Sosabowski, taking into consideration the strength of his unit revealed that it needed 170 glider pilots in September 1943, while in the Brigade the complement was short of 473 paratroopers of other ranks, so additional disposal of so many soldiers to retrain them as glider pilots was impossible. Source: Inspekcja Naczelnego Wodza w dn. 4-5 .IX. 1943 r. Notatka referowana dla Naczelnego Wodza, IPMGS, sign; A.V. 20\9–doc.13, p 1.

AS.51 Horsa Mk I. Arduous loading of a Jeep through port side cargo door. (IWM)

Due to expected use of the Parachute Brigade in combat I can not see possibility of training glider pilots from among Brigade's soldiers because:

- Glider pilot training takes about six months,
- The strength of the Brigade is much smaller than planned complement and regular depletion with lack of any reserves reduces it further day by day.
- However, there is possibility of forming a Department of Studies at the Brigade's Reserve Establishment, which would study the matter of glider-borne forces operations, preparing materials for further organization of glider-borne forces in Poland[96].

Indeed, the process of glider pilot training was long and demanding. Only after the theoretical ground training and three flights with an instructor, lasting 1.5 hours, was the trainee cleared for first solo flights and disengagements from the towplane at altitudes of 300-600 m. After having accumulated three flight hours of daylight training, then experience of adverse weather conditions, with tail – and crosswinds, with various weights of the glider began. After having mastered these skills in daylight, training at night followed. The training course ended with combat training flights, in simulated battlefield conditions[97].

Cargo hold of the Horsa glider.

---

96   *Odpowiedź na pismo Sztabu N.W. L.dz. 728/Op/W z dn. 10.V.44 r.* IPMGS, sign; A.V.20\17-doc.27.
97   T. Królikiewicz, *op. cit., p.* 42.

Before Operation "Market Garden" the headquarters of the 1st IPB requested 100 Horsa gliders for personnel and materiel transport. The headquarters of the Corps assigned only 45 Horsa Mk I gliders. True assignment for the 1st IPB in September 1944 should have comprised 99 Horsa and three Hamilcar gliders[98]. The gliders transporting the Poles belonged to RAF 38th Group[99].

The device used for locating the glider's CG on loading. Mémorial Pegasus (W. Zakrzewski)

Model of a Horsa glider after landing. Separated tail section and ramps, on which the Willys was unloaded. Museum Wings of Liberation (K. Nowicki)

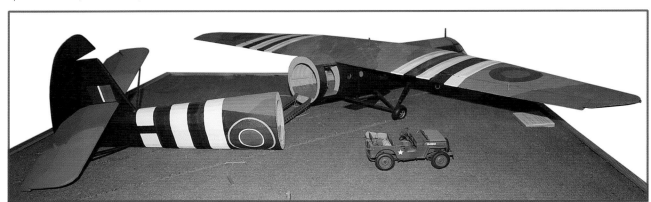

Mockup of a Horsa glider at Mémorial Pegasus, Benouville, France. (K. Nowicki)

98   J.H. Dyrda, op.cit., pp. 697-698.
99   W. Stasiak, *Uwagi i uzupełnienia do pracy Ryszarda Małaszkiewicza "Bitwa pod Arnhem"*, WPH issue 3, 1957, p. 275.

A Horsa towed by an Albermarle bomber. (wikipedia)

ARMSTRONG WHITWORTH WHITLEY

The first aircraft used by the forming Polish Parachute Brigade was a British bomber, the Armstrong Whitworth Whitley. This design was not very old (from 1934), but in the third year of the war it was outmoded. In 1941 in its primary role of heavy bomber the aircraft was obsolete, mainly due to its low speed and poor armament. Despite arrival of subsequent versions, up to Mk V, the Whitleys were replaced by other bomber types such as the Wellington or Halifax.

British parachute forces forming at that time were seeking for an aircraft for transport and dropping paratroopers. Virtually until the end of the war the British Army had no "true" transport aircraft of indigenous design for paratroopers, but initially Whitleys, among others, were used in this role, being suitable for transporting a paratrooper squad (10 men) over a long distance.

Due to the bomber's design the drop could be accomplished only through the opening in the floor. Its advantage was also the possibility of using the bomb bays to drop containers with equipment for the paratrooper squad or SOE operatives, which would soon become standard in all aircraft used for dropping paratroopers.

Particularly the last version, Mk V, powered by reliable Rolls-Royce Merlin engines could be used to carry and drop

parachute jumpers even into occupied Poland, as in the case of the first experimental flight of the first group of "Silent Unseen" and the their drop for the Armed Warfare Association resistance in Poland under operation Adolphus on 15/16 February 1941[100]. The drop was done "into the wild"[101], in the vicinity of the village of Dębowiec near Cieszyn.

A parajumper exiting a Whitley aircraft via the opening in the floor, the parachute is deploying. (Z. Wawer)

100 J. Tucholski, Cichociemni, Warsaw 1988, pp. 129-130. The group consisted of Maj. Stanisław Krzymowski „Kostka", rtm. Józef Zabielski „Żbik", bomb. Czesław Raczkowski „Orkan", the courier of Government Homeland Detachment.
101 The crew failed to find the destination spot near Włoszczowa and dropped the Silent Unseen over unknown terrain.

Paratroopers of the Polish 1st Parachute Brigade during practice jumps from Whitley aircraft, probably in 1942. (Z. Wawer)

Paratroopers of the 1st IPB before a practice jump from a Whitley at Ringway. (Z. Wawer)

Specifications[1]:
Whitley Mk V
Wingspan: 25.59 m
Length: 22.09 m
Height: 4.57 m
Bomb load: 3,178 kg
Powerplant: 2x Rolls-Royce Merlin V-12 liquid-cooled engines
Maximum speed: 358 km/h
Cruise speed: 298 km/h
Service ceiling: 5,363 m
Range: 2,661 km with 1,816 kg payload
Armament: one Browning .303 machine gun in the nose and four in the tail turret

1   http://www.raf.mod.uk/history/armstrongwhitworthwhitley.cfm – access: 12.12.2015.

DOUGLAS C-47 "SKYTRAIN" (DAKOTA)

This aircraft is a true American legend, recognizable even by the ignorant throughout the world, like the Willys Jeep and Colt 1911. Indeed, rarely does such a successful design appear that it remains in a very competitive market in this field for decades in virtually unaltered form.

The pattern for the best transport aircraft was its predecessor used in civil aviation – the Douglas DC-2[102]. When this aircraft entered widespread use in 1934 it revolutionized commercial air transport. However, several shortcomings of this aircraft (landing gear and brakes prone to failures) were eliminated in a subsequent version, the DC-3, that when the war broke out began to be adapted for the needs of military air transport.

The DC-3, which made its maiden flight in December 1935, was larger, faster and carried more payload than the DC-2. The military version could seat 28 soldiers with light equipment. The crew consisted of four airmen, pilot, co-pilot, navigator and wireless operator.

The main differences between the military (C-47) and civil version were large, two-section doors on the port side of the C-47, used for loading heavy equipment, including small vehicles, reinforced floor of the cargo hold and side benches for 28 soldiers. Some versions had additional fuel tanks in the cargo hold.

The large door, used for cargo loading, had an integral smaller door, used for dropping paratroopers. This system allowed for quick and safe drop of a paratrooper platoon, not only a squad. Moreover, later versions had provisions to carry airdropping containers beneath the fuselage and wings. Later also the tail section was modified to adapt the aircraft to the glider tug role.

A C-47 wearing the paint scheme from Operation Market Garden on an airfield. (P. Moszner)

102 Obviously the predecessor of both of them was the prototype DC-1, first flown in 1933; L. Davies, C-47 Skytrain in action, Carrollton 1995, p. 7.

The DC-2 operated by Polish Airlines LOT until the outbreak of the war. (US Congress Library).

The C-47 was the perfect plane for paratroopers. The cargo hold was spacious, allowed the paratroopers to stand upright. The paratrooper's equipment, taking up a lot of room, did not bother the others. The exit from the aircraft was easy and safe if the jump procedure – recoil from the doorstep – was observed. Static line jumps (the deployment occurred after the jump thanks to the line, attaching to the aircraft with one end, drawing off the canopy from the container) was facilitated thanks to the possibility of fastening individual static lines to steel lines stretched under the cargo hold ceiling.

The windows allowed for lighting up the darkness of the cargo hold. Embarking a smaller number of paratroopers, it was possible to take folding bicycles, baskets or containers and jettison them first. The stickman could easily control the exit of the paratroopers and jettisoning of equipment.

Disembarkation of paratroopers at a speed of about 300 km/h allowed for quick exit of the entire lineup without the

Inside a C-47. Polish paratroopers on their way to Arnhem. (Z. Wawer)

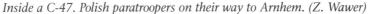

risk of paratroopers tangling together. It was a major advantage over the drop zone, when the aircraft was under enemy fire. Also disengaging paratroopers wounded by ground fire or those, whose parachutes opened prematurely aboard the aircraft due to pilot's dodging and withdrawing them from the drop did not disrupt the drop and took little time (the paratrooper could do it on his own).

The C-47 had the advantage of being capable of landing in rough terrain (an even meadow), not requiring a long take-off run. It was used during three "Wildhorn" (Polish: most – bridge) operations, when the C-47 landed at night in occupied Poland to take secret intelligence material (including V2 ballistic missile components) and exchange people.

For the operation at Arnhem 114 C-47 aircraft from USAAF 52nd Troop Carrier Wing were used[103].

Paratroopers of the 1st IPB embarking on a C-47 during Operation Market Garden. (Z. Wawer)

Specifications[1]:
Douglas C-47 Skytrain
Crew: four (pilot, co-pilot, navigator and wireless operator)
Wingspan: 29.41 m
Length: 19.43 m
Height: 5.18 m
Load capacity: 2,700 kg
Empty weight: 8,226 kg
Take-off weight: 14,061 kg
Powerplant: 2 × Pratt & Whitney R-1830-90C Twin Wasp 14-cylinder radial engines, 1,200 hp (895 kW) each
Maximum speed: 360 km/h
Cruise speed: 258 km/h
Service ceiling: 8,045 m
Range: 2,575 km

1   Pilot's Flight Operating Instruction. C-47 Airplane, Ohio 1943, p. 1; Pilot Training Manual for the Skytrain C-47, Washington 1945, p. 11.

103 W. Stasiak, *op. cit., p.275*

CHAPTER II
TROOP PARACHUTE DROPPING SYSTEM

During the Second World War in the British Army there were two systems of dropping parachute jumpers. Obviously this concerns paratrooper subunits, special forces units and SOE teams.

Chronologically the first was the method of dropping individual jumpers or small groups (up to 10 jumpers) through a specially prepared circular opening in an aircraft's floor, the so-called "hole".

In case of the British the situation was simple. It was enough to make an initial selection of recruits during conscription and assign those characterised by best psychological and physical features to airborne units. There, subjected to the training course relevant to their level of psychical fitness, they became paratroopers. The training, whose most important parts were parachute jumps, was progressed quickly with no regard for the unfit and injured dropping out.

In the allied Polish Parachute Brigade the situation was different. It initially consisted mostly of reserve officers, assigned to the Brigade by accident[1], who often had had no contact with any sport before the war[2]. This pool of soldiers, limited in numbers and initially lower than average, had to become a first-class force of the highest physical, psychological and moral qualifications. On the basis of physical exercises and on their own Ground Training Centre (Monkey Groove) at Largo House, the 1st Parachute Brigade developed a longer but less injury-producing method of improving the physical fitness of the soldiers, combined with preparations for parachute training.

In fact both British paratroopers, and the Polish unit which was being formed at that time, up until 1944 learned to parachute "through the hole" until a large number of C-47 transport aircraft arrived from the USA. Moreover, the Polish paratroopers, whose purpose had been initially supporting specialists in occupied Poland ("Silent Unseen") and then supporting a general uprising in the homeland, were obliged to get acquainted with this former system of parachuting, as more appropriate for designed purpose of the unit.

The soldiers of the Brigade, older and much less physically fit than the Britons, (to British parachute units athletes were primarily assigned) were undergoing their basic parachute training

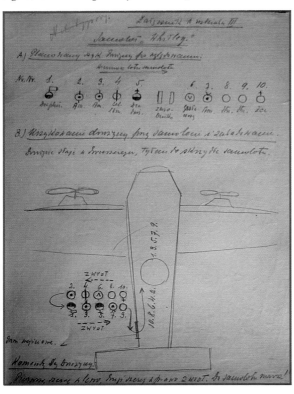

A copy of the appendix of parachute drill instruction for Whitley aircraft. The picture shows numbered soldiers of the parachute squad and their method of embarking on a Whitley aircraft. (IPMS)

---

1   It should be remembered that the 1st Parachute Brigade was formed on the basis of regular cadre brigade, after having taken away its most valuable soldiers, who reinforced the 1st Rifle Brigade. Only arduous work in accordance with indigenous training system ("Polish Method") and fierce struggle for replenishment of enlisted soldiers, regardless of their eligibility (this concerns the fact of posting of a group of about 100 soldiers, who had been expelled from previous units due to their low discipline). S. Sosabowski, *Droga wiodła ugorem*, London 1967, p. 118

2   *Ibidem*, s. 110.

not at the RAF parachuting school at Ringway, but at the indigenous Initial Training Centre at Largo, using self-made training devices for practising jumps through the opening in the aircraft's floor. An ingenuously adapted attic of a former horse barn at Largo House had openings in the floor, with sawn-off barrels inserted. The jump from the attic ended on the barn's floor 2.5 m, below on a layer of sand or straw (in later years on mattresses)[3]. On later stages of this exercise the jumps were made with the entire group sitting near the opening and taking position on the edge of it after the command "Action station!" After the command "Go" the trainee jumped[4]. The continuation of this training comprised similar exercises at the Ringway school and then jumps from a tethered observation balloon and from Whitley aircraft.

During this balloon training a group of five trainees with the instructor took seats in the balloon's nacelle. Before each jump the instructor checked whether the parachute harnesses were put on properly, paying most attention to the central single point release coupling. After this check the group of five trainee jumpers sat on the platform standing still on the ground. Static lines, drawing the canopy from the container, were fastened to a grip in the floor. The instructor strapped himself to the nacelle with a safety belt and gave the signal to start. The tethered balloon climbed to the planned altitude as the line unreeled from the winch's drum[5].

The climb of the balloon to jump altitude was slow and allowed for the jumpers to become adjusted to the space and altitude. In fact it was a serious stress, intensified by wind gusts and the nacelle rocking.

When the balloon reached the jump altitude (usually ca. 300 meters) the jumpers, according to the previously trained procedure, after the command "Action station" took in turns positions on the edge of the opening, to plummet into it after the command "Go!". The static line, fastened to the airplane's line with a snap hook, drew the parachute from the container. The ripcords securing the canopy in the deployment bag were ripped and the jumper could safely descend on the deployed parachute.

After having made several jumps from the balloon the next stage of training of individual paratroopers in this system of airdropping were jumps from a Whitley aircraft flying at altitude of about 500 m. When jumping from an aircraft through the opening in the floor the order of taking seats by the jumpers on embarking was important.

Having their numbers assigned the jumpers were informed by the instructor about where to sit on embarking. The instructor fastened the static line of each trainee's parachute to the line in the aircraft. The first to embark were odd numbers from the highest to the lowest and then even numbers in reverse order[6]. Even numbers were seated in the tail section and odd numbers on the other side of the opening, closer to the cockpit[7]. Embarkation was done always from the rear so as not to upset the aircraft's stability. The jump order was in accordance with assigned numbers.

After individual training, jumps in pairs were made. The first of the pair, after the command "Action station" sat on

Demonstrative photo of a jump through "the hole", a hatch in the airplane's floor. (MAK)

3   W. Borzemski, *op. cit.*, p. 9.

4   P. Bystrzycki, *Znak Cichociemnych*, Poznań 1991, p. 70

5   Polscy spadochroniarze..., p. 155.

6   Polscy spadochroniarze..., p. 157.

7   W. Stasiak, *op. cit., p.* 56.

Barrels mounted in the ceiling of an old stable – one of buildings at Largo House in Scotland. It was a training aid used in the Brigade's ground training facility, called "Monkey Grove". It was made by the Brigade's engineers. Postwar photograph (ZPS London).

the edge on the opening, shoving his legs into it and the other one took position across the hatch. After the instructor's command "go" the first one jumped, and the other one sat on the edge as quickly as possible and after the same command also plummeted into the opening. The training course ended with jumps in fives and finally of an entire squad of ten. The parachute drill and actions in both cases remained unchanged, but the jumps were made in quicker succession.

To further improve the skills of the jumpers an advanced training course was introduced. It included in addition to the airdrop of a squad from one aircraft, an airdrop of a platoon, i.e. 30 paratroopers from three aircraft flying in close formation[8]. The later part of the advanced course included a night jump from a balloon and night airdrop of a squad of ten from one aircraft. The advanced course lasted ten days, but later was combined with the basic training to allow completion of the course during a single stay at Ringway[9].

The system of jumping through "the hole" was inefficient (it was only changed by the arrival of C-47 aircraft) and dangerous. Accidents due to jumper's spinning after exit were frequent, especially when sliding down "the hole" the jumper hit his forehead against its edge.

It could result in the jumper tangling into the lines of a deploying parachute[10]. This situation was improved by a new method designed by the Polish instructor and commander of the Polish section at Ringway, 1st Lt Julian Gębołyś. This officer developed a new method of exiting the Whitley, with knees pressed to the chin. Such a position reduced the drag-inducing area and better protected the jumper against tumbling caused by the air stream. It had great significance, since it reduced the risk of tangling into the static line, drawing out the parachute from the container[11].

The system of exiting through "the hole" was abandoned in the 1st IPB when parachute units of the British Army received American C-47 Skytrain (Dakota) transport aircraft and began dropping paratroopers from them in 1944. At that time the Polish paratroopers were trained in the first system, but complemented their training with jumps in subunits and task forces from a Douglas C-47[12].

The latter system of airdropping paratroopers had several advantages to the former one. Above all, it was more efficient. The C-47 could carry 26 paratroopers with equipment and weapons or slightly fewer with Kit-bags and additional equipment jettisoned from the cargo hold (bicycles and baskets). Beneath the fuselage six CLT Mk III cargo containers or four containers and two Royal-Enfield 125 cc motorcycles in tubular airdropping crates could be carried. This was

---

8   P. Witkowski, Polskie jednostki powietrznodesantowe na Zachodzie, Warsaw 2009, p. 125.

9   Polscy spadochroniarze..., p. 142.

10   In the British Army and thus the 1st IPB backup parachutes were not used even during training jumps and parachute training course.

11   Z. H. Hrehorow Ostatni wzlot. pt. 2, "Spadochron" issue 101, 1985, p. 14.

12   The volunteers to combat in occupied homeland departed for Silent Unseen training centers, which became independent. After 1943 the Brigade was for them only the parachute training centre, preparing them to the parachute training course at Ringway.

a great increase in capability compared to the Whitley aircraft, carrying 10 paratroopers without the Leg Kit-bags and two airdropping containers. One can say that the Whitley carried a squad with equipment and weapons, and the Dakota a platoon.

Another advantage of jumping from a C-47 was the safety of the jumpers after the transition to the American system of jumping through side door. The paratroopers took seats along both sides of the cargo hold. After embarkation even numbers gave their neighbours sitting across the aisle one of two lines they were given before embarkation. On the stickman's (drop commander) command "Take-off position" the paratroopers had to take seats near the nose of the aircraft. Once in the air the pilot, who was the aircraft commander, gave the stickman the command "Travelling position" and the latter passed it to the paratroopers. On this command the paratroopers

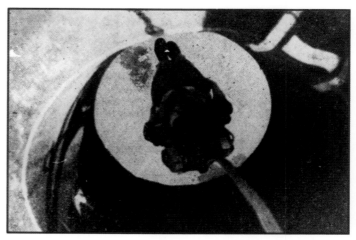

A paratrooper exiting through "the hole" in the floor.

spread and took positions for the flight to the drop zone, possibly lasting several hours. Twenty minutes before reaching the drop zone the pilot gave the stickman the command "prepare for action!", who passed it to the paratroopers. This could be replaced by switching on the green light over the door by the pilot, but only when it was agreed with the drop commander before take-off. The paratroopers stood up and fastened their static lines with snap hooks alternately to the steel wire stretched along the left side of the cargo hold. After having done this they made the final check of their harness and other items of equipment. The stickman reported the readiness for jump to the pilot. From that moment the entire group remained in readiness for the jump. Next actions were accomplished independently, the pilot switched off the light and the jumpers number 1 and 2 (first to depart) opened the door and secured it against closing during the airplane's manoeuvring. Five minutes before the drop the pilot gave the command "action station", confirmed by the stickman's "OK". A red light was switched on over the door and everybody waited for the green light, after which the equipment, such as bicycles and containers with parachutes, were jettisoned and then the paratroopers exited. If there was no additional equipment on board, the first paratrooper stood in the door, gripping the door frame with both hands. When the green light came on, which meant the command "Go", the jumper number one pushed with the left foot and both hands, exiting the airplane. Subsequent numbers approached the door, let the static line go and exited the aircraft[13].

Jumping from a Dakota was much more comfortable and pleasant for the paratroopers. They escaped head and face injuries, which often happening when jumping from a Whitley as result hitting their head against the opposite edge of the hatch.

The system of airdropping from a C-47 included several procedures, also emergency ones, to provide safety for the aircraft and jumpers. It was connected with take-off of the aircraft with jumpers (movable freight) and landing in emergency situations.

If during the flight, before reaching the drop zone, it became necessary to urgently drop of the jumpers, the drop commander and jumpers received from the pilot (in regulation situations) the command: "Section, section, prepare to abandon A/C". The pilot signalized it additionally with the door lights, flashing them alternately. This latter element was not essential and was used only when time allowed. After this command the drop commander (stickman) prepared the jumpers as after the command "Prepare for action" (taking positions and fastening the static lines to the steel line under the cargo hold ceiling), reporting the readiness to the pilot. After having received the report the pilot gave the command to exit[14].

During forced landing of a C-47 with jumpers aboard, the "Crash position" procedure was used. After such a command was given by the pilot, all jumpers aboard moved to the forward section of the cargo hold, close to the cockpit and got hold of elements of the airframe. If they previously had their static lines fastened, they had to unfasten them, and even take off their parachutes if time allowed, to be able to leave the aircraft as soon as possible after the crash landing, which often resulted in the aircraft catching fire[15].

Before ditching with jumpers aboard the pilot gave the command "Dinghy, dinghy, prepare for launching!". On this command the paratroopers had to take off parachutes and equipment, close the door and inflate their life vests. The soldiers gathered in the nose of the aircraft, grasping elements of the airframe. After ditching the door should be opened and the soldiers should leave the aircraft and board the inflatable rescue boat jettisoned from the aircraft (an item of equipment carried in flights over large expanses of water[16].

The method of airdropping developed for C-47 aircraft superseded the former one and was soon modified for use in various weather and tactical conditions. The framework within the airdrop of paratroopers by day and night was specified.

13   P.Witkowski, *op. cit., p.* 127.

14   Nauka przygotowania do działań bojowych..., p. 13.

15   *Ibidem*, p. 13.

16   *Ibidem*, p. 13

Parachutes of 1ˢᵗ IPB paratroopers deploying after a jump from a Whitley aircraft. (Wilkowski family archive).

The methods developed were used in three large airborne assaults during operations "Overlord", "Market Garden" and "Varsity".

The conclusions drawn from experience showed that the best formation for dropping a battalion was a formation of three airplanes, with an interval of 30 seconds to each another. In such cases the time needed for dropping a parachute battalion was 8-10 minutes. At night the most proper scheme was to airdrop in groups of 10-14 aircraft, with 10-minute intervals between individual formations. The time needed for dropping a battalion was then about one hour[17].

The formation carrying Polish paratroopers during Operation Market Garden consisted of 114 C-47 aircraft flying in four groups, three groups comprised 27 airplanes and the last one comprised 33 airplanes[18].

This system was simple and practical, but its frequent use could mean that the enemy eventually might learn to read it. Therefore for smaller units, such as the parachute brigade or its subunits, it was better to arrange their own code, valid only during a given operation, which would prevent the enemy from reading it.

Even in early 1944 (report from 30 March 1944) there were no dedicated subunits for marking the landing zones in the 1ˢᵗ IPB. This role was performed by soldiers of the Brigade's engineer company, but they had not been fully trained for it, contrary to British standards, entrusting these tasks to airborne engineers[19]. The situation did not change until the beginning of June of that year, when the 1ˢᵗ IPB became part of the British Airborne Corps. In the report for the Commander-in-Chief at that time in the Brigade were "untrained groups of parachute scouts [path-finders]" (original spelling)[20].

In Operation Market Garden the Polish Brigade did not use pathfinder teams, because according to plans it was to land in an area controlled by subunits of the British 1ˢᵗ Airborne Division, whose drop zone preparation and marking teams were initially to perform this role. In the changing operational situation (lack of communication with the 1ˢᵗ Airborne Division, change of departure date of the 1ˢᵗ IPB, change of the drop zone to one located near the village of Driel) and due to the fact that the airdrop was made in daylight (at Driel about 1720 hours – PW) the Brigade's own pathfinder teams were not used. Probably the area of the drop zone, to be used in good visibility, had so many characteristic features (the river, village of Driel, railroad) that there was no need to mark it.

However the article written by Jerzy Dyrda, a 1ˢᵗ IPB officer, indicates rather that the drop zone was to be marked by British paratrooper teams, who had failed to arrive. Jerzy Dyrda comments on this situation: "In the drop zone there was neither the cover of the British 1ˢᵗ Airborne Division, nor its pathfinders and means of transport."[21]

---

17 *Ibidem*, p. 11.

18 J. Dyrda, *op. cit.*, p. 697; Annex 5.

19 Weryho, *Notatka z inspekcji kompanii saperów Brygady Spad.*, IPMS, sign. A.V.20/31/15-doc.25, p. 149.

20 S. Sosabowski, *Sprawozdanie o stanie wyszkolenia i gotowości bojowej 1.Samodz. Brygady Spadochr.*, IPMS, sign. A.V.20/31/15-doc. 25, p.155.

21 J. Dyrda, *op. cit.*, p. 702.

Pathfinders are marking the drop zone using signaling canvas sheets.

Due to the new organizational scheme of the 1st IPB, from 11 January 1945 an independent pathfinder company, comprising three platoons, was formed[22].

The drop zones were selected in terms of their tactical usefulness, enabling use of the main asset of the paratroopers – surprise. Other parameters taken into consideration in selection of the drop zone were the length, airspeed at which the airdrop was made, number of dropped paratroopers and amount of equipment, number of exits (doors and hatches). Moreover, in specifying the width of the drop zone, the height from which the drop was made and wind speed were taken into consideration[23].

Finding and marking the drop zones were the tasks of pathfinder squads. In the 1st IPB, as in all other parachute units, such a group existed whose task was to be dropped usually about one hour before the drop of the main force of their own unit and to mark the drop zone or zones in which the main force would land. Sometimes this was an extremely difficult task, because as the experience of the night airdrop in Normandy showed, the pathfinders did not land in the drop zone but had to find the drop zone first, and then mark it. Also the results of inspections of the exercises of the 1st IPB by officers of the Commander-in-Chief staff mentioning unsatisfactory skills of the Brigade's pathfinders.

By night the landing/drop zones were marked by fires lit in the middle, flashlights or flares. By day 5x1 m canvas sheets were laid in a prearranged shape (e.g. X or L)[24]. In May 1944 the airborne forces adopted the signal code for aerial observers, using the following configuration of signal panels meaning[25]:

22 Commander: Capt. Stefan Malanek, deputy commander: 1st Lt Stanisław Nocoń, platoon commanders respectively: 2nd Lt Czesław Smółczyński, 2nd Lt Jan Czarski, 2nd Lt Leon Ziółkowski. See: S. Jachnik, *Rozkaz zatwierdzający obsady personalne stanowisk w 1.SBS*, IPMS, sign. A.V.20/17-doc 1, s. 2.

23 *Nauka przygotowania do działań bojowych...*, p. 8.

24 *Ibidem* p. 9.

25 J. Bouchery, *The British Soldier. From D-Day to VE-Day, vol.1*, Paris 2001, p. 137.

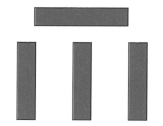

Request for food supplies

Request for ammunition to the light weapon

Request for drinking water

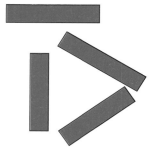

Request for a medications

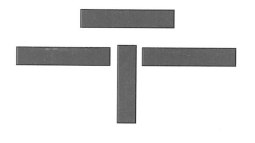

Request for fuel and oil

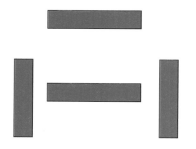

Goals have been achieved

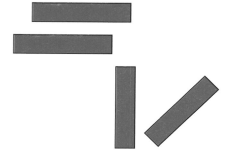

OK, land here

We are under attack

Do not land or drop here

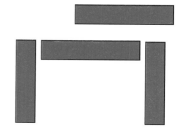

OK, drop here

ACKNOWLEDGEMENTS

I thank all individual persons, organizations and institutions for making their collections, knowledge and assistance accessible, thanks to which this book could be written[1]:

♦ Jarosław Kaleczyc
♦ Witold Zakrzewski
♦ Airborne Museum "Hartenstein" in Oosterbeek (AM),
♦ Bernhard Angerer – *Embacher-Collection,*
♦ Geert Versleyen – *Yesterdays Antique Motorcycles,*
♦ The Polish Institute and Sikorski Museum in London,
♦ The Home Army Museum Cracow (MAK),
♦ Warsaw Rising Museum (MPW),
♦ Polish Army Museum in Warsaw (MWP),
♦ Ox and Bucks
♦ Marek Wroński – Museum of Tarnowskie Góry Institute,
♦ Jacek Dziedziela – Former Airborne Soldiers Association "Red Berets",
♦ Piotr Wybraniec – Airborne and Special Forces Museum, Wisła,

Re-enactment groups:
♦ 1st Independent Parachute Brigade Reenactment Group at 12th Detachment of Polish Parachuting Association, Łódź (GRH 1SBS),
♦ 1st Independent Commando Company Reenactment Group, *"No 10 Commando" Swarzędz* (GRH 1SKC),
♦ Re-enactment Association "To you, Fatherland" (TO).

Private collectors:
♦ Artur Pilski,
♦ Bob Adams,
♦ Dick Timmerman (DT),
♦ Erik van Tilbeurgh (EvT),
♦ Grzegorz Zając (GZ),
♦ Jan Poortman,
♦ Jan Wilkowski,
♦ Jarosław Kaleczyc,
♦ Peter Zijlstra,
♦ Steven Duda,
♦ Witold Zakrzewski,
♦ Wojciech Radecki,
♦ Zbigniew Wawer.

---

1 In brackets are given initials of individual persons and institutions, to which the exhibits and photo copyright belong. Photographs in the book without specified copyright belong to collection of the 1st Independent Parachute Brigade Reenactment Group (including M. Różyński, M. Szparagowski and P. Witkowski)

APPENDICES

ANNEX 1

List of vehicles of the 1st IPB on 16 June 1944[1]

Unit and its location	Vehicle type	Quantity	Make	Transferred to:	In possession and to be retained by unit (quantity, type and number)	Total
1st IPB HQ – Leven, Fife.	Motorcycle solo 125 cc	12	Royal Enfield			12
	Motorcycle solo 350 cc	5	Ariel			5
	Car 4x2 Lt. Utility.	4	Austin		1 – Austin 4888240.	5
	Car 4x2 Hy. Utility.	–	–			2
	Truck 15-cwt 4x2 G.S	2	Ford (British)		2 – Ford: 714034, 767350	2
	Lorry 3-ton. 4x2 G.S	1	Bedford			1
Airborne Light Artillery Squadron – Leven, Fife.	Motorcycle solo 125 cc.	14	Royal Enfield			14
	Motorcycle solo 350 cc	21	Ariel		1 – Austin 4424913.	21
	Car 4x2 Lt. Utility.	–	–		3 – Willys: 1165580, 4231609, 430361	1
	Car 5-cwt 4x4.	38	Ford/Willys			41
	Truck 15-owt 4x2 GS	2	Ford (British)		1 – Ford 4962821.	3
	Tanker 15-cwt 4x2 200 gal. (909 l)	1	Bedford			1
	Truck 3-ton. 4x4 GS Trailer 10-cwt 2-wh.	4	Ford (Canada)		6 – Trailers: 5279544, 5279543, 5279576, 5279606, 5279551, 5279547.	4
	Trailer 10-cwt 2-wh. (Lightweight G.S)	29	Trailer			35
	Motorcycle solo 350 cc	31	Ariel			31
	Car 4x2 Lt. Utility. Car 5-cwt 4x4.	1 / 23	Austin / Ford/Willys		6 – Willys: 4232267, 1165570, 4219059, 4230751, 4231208, 4231698.	1 / 29
Airborne Anti-tank Squadron – Leven, Fife.	Truck 15-cwt 4x2 GS	1	Ford (British)		1 – Ford 4507010	2
	Tanker 15-cwt 4x2 200 gal. (909 l)	1	Bedford			1
	Truck 3-ton. 4x4 G.S	3				3
	Trailer 10-cwt 2-wh. (Lightweight G.S)	7	Ford (Canada) Trailers		6 – Trailers: 5279610, 5279531, 5279548, 527953, 5279549, 5279542.	13
Airborne Engineer Company – Leven, Fife.	Motorcycle solo 125 c.c. (in lieu of Welbike)	14	Royal Enfield			14
	Motorcycle solo 350 c.c.	2	Ariel			2
	Car 4x2 Lt. Utility.	1	Austin			1
	Truck 3-ton. 4x2 G.S	1	Bedford			1

1 According to: Urgent memorandum. Subject: "B" Vehicles, IPMS, sign.: A.V20/31/15 – doc. 23.

Unit and its location	Vehicle type	Quantity	Make	Transferred to:	In possession and to be retained by unit (quantity, type and number)	Total
Airborne Signals Company – Leven, Fife.	Motorcycle solo 125 c.c. (in lieu of *Welbike*)	7	Royal Enfield			7
	Motorcycle solo 125 cc	4	Royal Enfield			4
	Motorcycle solo 350 cc	9	Ariel			9
	Car 4x2 Lt. Utility.	3	Austin			3
	Car 5-cwt 4x4.	5	Ford/Willys			5
	Truck 15-cwt 4x2 G.S.	–	–		3 – Ford: 4846014, 4846019, 492814.	3
	Truck 3-ton. 4x4 G.S.	1	Ford (Can)			1
	Trailer 10-cwt 2wh .G.S.	5	Trailer			5
	Trailer lightweight 2wh (in lieu of 10-cwt)	1	Trailer lightweight			1
1st Parachute Battalion – Leven, Fife.	Motorcycle solo 125 cc	18	Royal Enfield			18
	Motorcycle solo 350 cc	2	Ariel			2
	Car 4x2 Lt. Utility.	–	–		1 – Austin 4888053.	1
	Car 4x2 Hy. Utility.	–	–		1 – Ford 4767353.	1
	Car 5-cwt 4x4.	4	Ford/Willys			4
	Truck 15-cwt 4x2 GS	1	Ford (British)			1
	Tanker 15-cwt 4x2 200 gal. (909 l)	–	Bedford			
	Lorries 3-ton 4x2 G.S.	8	Bedford			8
2nd Parachute Battalion – Leven, Fife.	Motorcycle solo 125 cc	18	Royal Enfield			18
	Motorcycle solo 350 cc	2	Ariel			2
	Car 4x2 Lt. Utility.	–	–	1st Para Battalion 1 – Austin 4888229		1
	Car 4x2 Hy. Utility.	1	Ford/Willys			1
	Car 5-cwt 4x4.	–	–		1 – Ford 4767329	1
	Truck 15 –cwt 4x2 GS	4	Ford (British)			4
	Tanker 15-cwt 4x2 200 gal. (909 l)	–	Bedford		1 – Bedford Z4871291	1
	Truck 3-ton. 4x2 GS	8	Bedford			8
3rd Parachute Battalion – Leven, Fife.	Motorcycle solo 125 cc	18	Royal Enfield		1 – Bedford Z4871294	18
	Motorcycle solo 350 cc	2	Ariel			2
	Car 4x2 Lt. Utility.	–	–	1st Para Battalion. 1 – Austin 4888224 Airborne Medical Company 1 – Ford 4767338		1
	Car 4x2 Hy. Utility.	1	–			1
	Car 5-cwt 4x4.	1	Ford/Willys			1
	Truck 15-cwt 4x2 G.S	4	Ford (British)			4
	Tanker 15-cwt 4x2 200 gal. (909 l)	–				1
	Truck 3-ton. 4x2 2G.S.	8	Bedford			8

Unit and its location	Vehicle type	Quantity	Make	Transferred to:	In possession and to be retained by unit (quantity, type and number)	Total
Airborne Medical Company – Leven, Fife.	Motorcycle solo 125 cc	11	Royal Enfield			11
	Motorcycle solo 350 cc	6	Ariel			6
	Car 4x2 Hvy. Utility.	-	–	1 – Ford 467359		1
	Car 5-cwt 4x4.	5	Ford/Willys			5
	Truck 15-cwt 4x2 GS	4	Ford (British)			4
	Truck 3-ton. 4x2 G.S.	1	Bedford			1
	Heavy ambulance	7	Austin	1 – Austin 26907		8
Transport and Supply Company – Leven, Fife.	Motorcycle solo 350 cc	19	Ariel			19
	Car 4x2 Lt.	4	Austin		1 – Austin 4888234	5
	Utility Car 4x2 Hvy.	-	–		1 – Ford 4767337	1
	Utility Truck 15-cwt 4x2 GS.	2	Ford (British)		2 – Ford 4507020, 4846018	4
	Tanker 15-cwt 4x2 200 gal. (909 l)	3	Bedford			3
	Truck 3-ton. 4x2 G.S	41	Bedford			41
	Truck 3-ton.4x2 f/w6Y&2Z bins.	1	Bedford			1
	Truck 3-ton 6x4 B/Down	1	Leyland (old version)			1

ANNEX 2

Complement and actual strength of the 1st IPB on 19.09.1944[1]

Subunit	Brigade establishment			Strength recorded on 15.06. 1944			Actual strength on 19.09. 1944			Equipment and armament by quantity
	officers	other ranks	total	officers	other ranks	total	officers	other ranks	total	
Headquarters + guard platoon	26/6[1]	53/17	79/23	26/6	49/17	75/23	26/6	49/17	75/23	40 – revolvers, 3 – Bren, 2 – PIAT, 30 – rifles (SMLE) and 65 – Sten, 2 – Passenger Cars, 4 – trucks, 6 – Willys, 4 – motorcycles, 5 – bicycles
Military police platoon	1/ –	15/ –	16/ –	1/ –	11/2	12/2	1/ –	11/2	12/2	10 – revolvers, 10 – Sten, 1 – Motorcycle, 10 – bikes (perhaps Welbikes were meant –PW)
Defensive scouting squad	–	7/1	7/1	–	7/1	7/1	–	7/1	7/1	8 – revolvers, 7 – Sten
Military court	3/ –	4/ –	7/ –	-/2	-/4	-/6	-/2	-/4	-/6	7 – revolvers

1 J. Kamiński, Operacja wojsk alianckich "Market Garden", Military Historic Research Bureau, sign. XII/12/89, pp. 3-5.

Subunit	Brigade establishment			Strength recorded on 15.06.1944			Actual strength on 19.09.1944			Equipment and armament by quantity
	officers	other ranks	total	officers	other ranks	total	officers	other ranks	total	
Field post	-/1	-/4	-/5	-	-/1	-/1	-	-/1	-/1	5 – pistols, 1 – Willys, 2 – bicycles
Transport and supply company - administrative platoon - transport platoon - repair platoon - airborne supply platoon	7/6	58/84	65/90	7/5	58/44	65/49	7/5	58/44	65/49	5 – revolvers, 60 – Sten, 50 –rifle (SMLE) 28 – trucks, 10 – willys, 7 – motorcycles, 10 – bicycles
Airborne Signals Company Command platoon „A" – communication with the superior and one neighbor, „J" – radio communication with one subordinate „C" – cable communication, „D" – motorcycle and bicycle messengers	7/1	103/6	110/7	7/1	103/6	110/7	7/1	94/6	101/7	20 – revolvers, 80 –Sten, 30 –rifles (SMLE) "A" – R-19 – 4 (up to 55 km), R-22 (12-25 km, on reflected 300 km). "J" R-22 – 12,R-18 – 8 (16 km) "C" – telephone exchange-2, telephones – 12, trucks – 4, Willys-5, motorcycles-6, bicycles-10.
Airborne Medical Company 3 paramedic teams 2 surgeon teams	10/1	103/8	113/9	10/1	103/8	113/9	10/1	103/8	113/9	11 – revolvers, 8 – ambulances, 4-trucks, 6 – Willys, 12-motorcycles, 18-bicycles, leased surgeon (with clearance for surgical operations with transfusion)
Airborne Engineer Company 2 officer patrols 3 platoons comprising 3 squads each	15/ –	152/6	167/6	11/ –	130/6	141/6	11/ –	130/6	141/6	25-revolvers, 9-PIAT, 9-BREN, 170-Sten, explosives: plastic and anti-tank mines 500, Willys-6, Trucks-5, motorcycles-12, inflatable boats-6.
1ˢᵗ Parachute Battalion - Command company - Administrative platoon - Signals platoon - Heavy weapons platoon + 3 companies comprising 3 platoons consisting of 3 squads	46/6	519/42	565/48	43/4	368/22	411/26	42/4	344/22	386/26	Mortar M3-6, Mortar M2-27, PIAT-18, BREN-27, Sten and SMLE – 600, revolvers-60, R-22 – 5, R-18-1, R-36 – 48, trucks-5, Willys-10, motorcycles-5, bicycles-20.
2ⁿᵈ Parachute Battalion (order of battle as above)	46/6	519/42	565/48	46/6	394/22	440/28	45/6	364/22	409/28	As above
3ʳᵈ Parachute Battalion (order of battle as above)	46/6	519/42	565/48	45/6	407/22	452/28	43/6	372/22	415/28	As above

Subunit	Brigade establishment			Strength recorded on 15.06.1944			Actual strength on 19.09.1944			Equipment and armament by quantity
	officers	other ranks	total	officers	other ranks	total	officers	other ranks	total	
Airborne Light Artillery Squadron headquarters signals platoon 2 batteries with 4 guns each	14/–	124/–	138/–	11/–	125/2	136/2	11/–	125/–	136/–	Howitzers 75mm – 8, BREN – 5, PIAT-3, STEN – 60, SMLE – 60, revolver – 30, artillery rounds 1,600, Willys-28, motorcycles – 18
Airborne Light Artillery Squadron – headquarters – signals platoon – 2 batteries with 4 guns each	14/–	124/–	138/–	11/–	125/2	136/2	11/–	125/–	136/–	Howitzers 75mm – 8, BREN – 5, PIAT-3, STEN – 60, SMLE – 60, revolver – 30, artillery rounds 1,600, Willys-28, motorcycles – 18
Airborne Anti-tank Squadron	8/–	153/–	161/–	8/–	126/6	134/6	8/–	126/6	134/6	R-22 –10, R-18 – 5, gun-16, in action 15, BREN – 10, revolver – 24, Sten-140, Willys-42, motorcycles-10, artillery rounds 1,600.
Total	235/36	2342/253	2577/289	221/33	1881/200	2102/200	217/33	1783/165	2000/198	x

ANNEX 3

List of equipment carried from Great Britain to the Continent by the 1st naval component of the 1st IPB for Operation Market Garden and equipment returning from the operation within the 1st naval component[1]

Unit	Cars 4-seat	Cars 2-seat	5-cwt Jeeps	Trailers for Jeeps	Trucks 15-cwt	Trucks 15-cwt (Water Tanker)	Trucks 3-ton	Ambulances	Canteens	Mobile workshops	guns	Motorcycles
HQ	1/1	-/-	-/-	-/-	2/2	-/-	2/2	-/-	2/1	-/-	-/-	5/-
Field materiel depot	-/-	1/1	3/2	32	11	1/1	2/2	-/-	-/-	-/-	-/-	-/-
1.Para Battalion	1/1	-/-	1/1	2/2	-/-	1/1	6/6	-/-	-/-	-/-	-/-	-/-
2. Para Battalion	1/1	-/-	1/1	1/1	-/-	1/1	6/6	-/-	-/-	-/-	-/-	-/-
3. Para Battalion	1/1	-/-	1/1	1/1	-/-	1/1	6/6	-/-	-/-	-/-	-/-	-/-
Light Artillery Squadron	-/-	-/-	1/1	-/-	-/-	1/1	3/3	-/-	-/-	-/-	1/-	-/-
Anti-tank Squadron	-/-	-/-	2/9	2/2	-/-	-/-	2/2	-/-	-/-	-/-	2/9	-/-

1 *Wykaz pojazdów mechanicznych I.rzutu morskiego w drodze na Kontynent*, IPMS, sygn.:A.V.20/31/46-dok.12, k. 63; *Wykaz pojazdów mechanicznych I.rzutu morskiego w drodze powrotnej*, IPMS, sign.:A.V.20/31/46-doc.12, c. 64. Numbers in the table indicate respectively: *there / back.*

List of vehicles carried from Great Britain to the Continent by the 2nd naval component of the 1st IPB for Operation Market Garden[1]

Unit	Cars 4-seat	Cars 2-seat	5-cwt Jeeps	Trailers for Jeeps	Trucks 15-cwt	Trucks 15-cwt (Water Tanker)	Trucks 3-ton	Ambulances	Canteens	Mobile workshops	guns	Motorcycles
Signals company	-/-	-/-	1/5	2/6	2/2	-/-	1/1	-/-	-/-	-/-	-/-	-/-
Engineer company	-/-	-/-	-/-	-/-	1/1	-/-	4/4	-/-	-/-	-/-	-/-	-/-
Medical company	1/1	-/-	-/-	-/-	2/2	-/-	1/1	7/6	-/1	-/-	-/-	-/-
Transport platoon	-/-	-/-	6/6	7/7	1/1	-/-	24/23	-/-	-/-	-/-	-/-	1/-
Repair platoon	-/-	-/-	3/3	3/3	1/1	1/1	4/4	-/-	-/-	2/2	-/-	-/-
Total	5/5	1/1	19/29	21/24	10/10	6/6	61/60	7/6	2/2	2/2	3/9	6/11

Jeep	Austin	standard	Trailers	Guns	Trucks 15-cwt	Trucks 3-ton	Motorcycles	Ford passenger	Ambulance	Motorcycle R-E 125 cc	15-cwt (Water Tanker)	Mobile workshop	Total
55	5	2	50	8	27	17	43	2	1	1	3	1	215

1 *Sprawozdanie z podróży służbowej II-go rzutu morskiego*, IPMS, sign.:A.V.20/31/48-doc.1, c. 2. In the second column it was not specified what type of Austin is concerned, probably Austin 10 HP. The third column "standard" may concern Humber FWD or Hillman 10 HP cars. However, it is only author's hypothesis.

ANNEX 4

Glider component of the 1st IPB during Operation Market Garden

1st glider batch of the 1st IPB, 18 September[1]

Glider number	Complement[2]	Subunit	Loadout	Airfield of departure	Landing place[3]
890	LCpl. Gieniec Józef LCpl. Rogoziński Jan PFC Gimel Roman Pvt. Piekarski Wiktor	Airborne Anti-tank Squadron	Jeep + trailer, 60 artillery rounds, 2 motorcycles, miscellanous[4].	Manston	LZ "X"
891	2nd Lt Mleczko Władysław, LCpl. Zawistowski Stefan, PFC Chartonowicz Kazimierz, PFC Skaczko Józef	Airborne Anti-tank Squadron	Jeep + trailer, 60 artillery rounds, 2 motorcycles, miscellanous.	Manston	LZ "X"
892	Cpl Officer Cadet Pogoda Marian, PFC Dejhofos Grzegorz	Airborne Anti-tank Squadron	Jeep + 6-pounder gun, 18 artillery rounds, Bren machine gun + ammunition, engineering equipment, R-18 wireless set, medical equipment.	Manston	LZ "X"
893	Cpl Nowak Józef, PFC Szabała Bazyli	Airborne Anti-tank Squadron	Jeep + 6-pounder gun, 18 artillery rounds, Bren machine gun + ammunition.	Manston	LZ "X"

1 Glider numbers, assignment to subunits, airfield of departure of the gliders: *Rozkaz Organizacyjny – Dział Powietrzny, Ldz.1587/OP/Tjn/44.* from 13 September 1944, IPMS, sign. A.V.20/31/28-1, p. 2 – *Cz. 4. Rzut szybowcowy* (table).

Glider number	Complement[2]	Subunit	Loadout	Airfield of departure	Landing place[3]
894	Cpl Kądzioła Franciszek PFC Pulikowski Jan	Airborne Anti-tank Squadron	Jeep + 6-pounder gun, 18 artillery rounds, Bren machine gun + ammunition.	Manston	LZ "X"
895	kpr. Romaniszyn Józef kan. Tereszczuk Jan	Airborne Anti-tank Squadron	Jeep + 6-pounder gun, 18 artillery rounds, Bren machine gun + ammunition.	Manston	LZ "X"
896	LCpl Wolski Władysław, PFC Kurowski Władysław	Airborne Anti-tank Squadron	Jeep + 6-pounder gun, 18 artillery rounds, Bren machine gun + ammunition.	Manston	LZ "X"
897	Cpl Kluz Henryk, PFC Napolski Kazimierz	Airborne Engineer Company	Jeep: One crate of *gammon bombs*, 1 *Bren* machine gun+ 400 rounds. 1 rifle + 110 rounds, one box of anti-vehicle mines + 2 trailers: 400 *Hawkins No 75 mines*, 16 PIAT rounds, 36 M-2 mortar rounds, 2 *dinghies*, 2500 rounds for *Bren* machine gun.	Manston	LZ "X"
898	kpr. Wojakowski Stanisław st. sap. Wesołowski Bronisław	Airborne Engineer Company	Jeep: One crate of *gammon bombs*, 1 *Bren* machine gun+ 400 rounds. 1 rifle + 110 rounds, one box of anti-vehicle mines + 2 trailers: 400 *Hawkins No 75 mines*, 16 PIAT rounds, 36 M-2 mortar rounds, 2 *dinghies*, 2500 rounds for *Bren* machine gun.	Manston	LZ "X"
899[5]	Capt Zwolański Ludwik, Capt Maćkowiak Alfons Święcicki Marek – war correspondent Signals Company patrol: Lcpl Officer Cadet Pająk Stanisław, PFC Kuczewski Władysław, Pvt. Paulski Bolesław	HQ forward detachment	Jeep: R-22 wireless set, 300 W battery charger, 6 gallons of petrol, Trailer: 2 R-22 wireless set, 6 batteries, 4 gallons of petrol, 2 gallons of oil, signal sheets, 2 tents, 300 W charger.	Manston	LZ "X"

2nd glider batch of the 1st IPB, 19 September 1944

Glider number	Complement	Subunit	Loadout	Airfield of departure	Landing place
120	2nd Lt Grabowski Walenty, Pvt Biernat Ignacy, PFC.Oprych Józef, Pvt Rapacewicz Witold	Airborne Anti-tank Squadron	Jeep+ trailer, 60 artillery rounds, 2 motorcycles, miscellaneous	Tarrant-Rushton	LZ "L"
121	Cpl officer cadet Frodyma Władysław, LCpl Tymoszuk Adam, LCpl Tylek Stefan, Pvt Gorzko Stanisław	Airborne Anti-tank Squadron	Jeep+ trailer, 60 artillery rounds, 2 motorcycles, miscellaneous	Tarrant-Rushton	LZ "L"
122	Cpl Pawłowski Stanisław, LCpl Hajduk Wacław, Pvt Dziekiewicz Jan, Pvt Rożkowiec Aleksander	Airborne Anti-tank Squadron	Jeep+ trailer, 60 artillery rounds, 2 motorcycles, miscellaneous	Tarrant-Rushton	LZ "L"

2   Complements of gliders and load carried into combat – according to loadsheets for glider components of individual subunits: IPMS, sign. A.V.20/31/29 and based on accounts and studies.

3   Landing locations of gliders of the first Polish batch according to: Tugs and Gliders to Arnhem, Eijsden 2000

4   The term „miscellaneous" applies only to the Airborne Anti-tank Squadron. It denotes equipment, which could be useful in combat and which could be loaded aboard the glider to attain its allowed load capacity. These usually were Bren machine guns with ammunition, medical equipment, gunsmith equipment, fuel supply, spare wheel for the gun, R-18 and R-38 wireless sets with spare batteries, ammunition for Sten submachine guns. See: W. Mleczko, Odtworzenie Form "B" glider, IPMS, sign. A.V.20/38/29-8, c.13.

5   According to: Załadowanie ludzi i sprzętu na szybowce oraz szyk w nalocie. Kwatera Główna, IPMS, sign.V.20/31/31-doc.5; Zestawienie rzutu szybowcowego op. MARKET, IPMS, sign. A.V.20/31/29-doc. 10.

Glider number	Complement	Subunit	Loadout	Airfield of departure	Landing place
123	Ssgt Jędrych Franciszek, Pvt Chmielewski Wiktor, Pvt Gregorek Zygmunt, Pvt Serba Franciszek	**Airborne Anti-tank Squadron**	Jeep+ trailer, 45 artillery rounds, 39 artillery rounds on the floor in lieu of motorcycles, miscellaneous	Tarrant-Rushton	LZ "L"
124	2nd Lt Wróblewski Adolf, PFC Gałązka Henryk, PFC Semczyszyn Stefan, PFC Węgiel Józef	**Airborne Anti-tank Squadron**	Jeep+ trailer, 60 artillery rounds, 2 motorcycles, miscellaneous	Tarrant-Rushton	LZ "L"
125	LCpl Malinowski Jan, LCpl Matuszczak Stefan LCpl Wiewiórski Mikołaj LCpl Kołaniakowski Wacław	**Airborne Anti-tank Squadron**	Jeep+ trailer, 60 artillery rounds, 2 motorcycles, miscellaneous	Tarrant-Rushton	LZ "L"
126	Sgt Maślorz Piotr, Pvt Nowak Kazimierz	**Airborne Anti-tank Squadron**	Jeep + 6-pounder gun, 18 artillery rounds, Bren machine gun + ammunition.	Tarrant-Rushton	The glider had its tail shot off by German anti-aircraft artillery and crashed near Sint Michielsgestel. Netherlands[6].
127	Cpl. Horodeczny Stanisław, PFC Karczyński Józef	**Airborne Anti-tank Squadron**	Jeep + 6-pounder gun, 18 artillery rounds, Bren machine gun + ammunition.	Tarrant-Rushton	LZ "L"
128	LCpl Parzuchowski Polikarp, LCpl Siniak Mateusz	**Airborne Anti-tank Squadron**	Jeep + 6-pounder gun, 18 artillery rounds, Bren machine gun + ammunition.	Tarrant-Rushton	LZ "L"
129	Cpl Pyliński Emanuel kan. Jóźwik Bronisław	**Airborne Anti-tank Squadron**	Jeep + 6-pounder gun, 18 artillery rounds, Bren machine gun + ammunition.	Tarrant-Rushton	LZ "L"
130	LCpl Rycina Antoni Pvt Kiełbasa Stanisław	**Airborne Anti-tank Squadron**	Jeep + 6-pounder gun, 18 artillery rounds, Bren machine gun + ammunition.	Tarrant-Rushton	The towing line was severed by German AAA fire. The glider force landed on no man's land 30 km short of the target. The crew were taken prisoner by Germans[7].
131	1st Lt Halpert Jerzy, PFC. Kabat Roman, PFC Lenc Władysław, PFC Nowosielski Jerzy, officer cadet Nosecki Stanisław – war correspondent	**Airborne Anti-tank Squadron**	Jeep+ trailer, 60 artillery rounds, 2 motorcycles, miscellaneous	Tarrant-Rushton	LZ "L"
132	Cpl Laszkiewicz Stefan, Pvt Młodowski Aleksander	**Airborne Anti-tank Squadron**	Jeep + 6-pounder gun, 18 artillery rounds	TarrantRushton	LZ "L"
133	Cpl Trochim Edward, PFC Uzłowski Aleksander	**Airborne Anti-tank Squadron**	Jeep + 6-pounder gun, 18 artillery rounds	Tarrant-Rushton	After having flown into clouds the glider pilot lost the towplane from view, disengaged and landed at Bredene, 5 km northeast of Ostend[8].
134	Cpl Multan Stanisław, Pvt Sońko Józef	**Airborne Anti-tank Squadron**	Jeep + 6-pounder gun, 18 artillery rounds	Tarrant-Rushton	LZ "L"
135	LCpl Officer Cadet Zjawin Zbigniew, Pvt Barowicz Adam	**Airborne Anti-tank Squadron**	Jeep + 6-pounder gun, 18 artillery rounds	Tarrant-Rushton	LZ "L"
136	LCpl Pawlaczyk Edmund Pvt Kocaj Piotr	**Airborne Anti-tank Squadron**	Jeep + 6-pounder gun, 18 artillery rounds	Tarrant-Rushton	LZ "L"
137	LCpl Okoń Józef , PFC Kołodyński Stefan, PFC Ratowski Józef, PFC. Szołtyski Zygmunt	**Airborne Anti-tank Squadron**	Jeep+ trailer, 60 artillery rounds., 2 motorcycles, miscellaneous	Tarrant-Rushton	LZ "L"

Glider number	Complement	Subunit	Loadout	Airfield of departure	Landing place
138	2nd Lt Sawicki Stefan, PFC Koczan Wacław	1st Parachute Battalion	Jeep: *Bren* machine gun + 400 rounds, R-18 wireless set, Battalion HQ office, 2,600 rounds of ammunition. 2 trailers: 5 *Vickers* machine guns+5,000 rounds, 42 HE rounds for M-3 mortar, 3,600 rounds of ammunition	Tarrant-Rushton	LZ "L"
139	PFC Kopeć Stanisław PFC Zajączkowski Antoni, Pvt Markowski Stanisław	1st Parachute Battalion	Jeep: *Bren* machine gun + 500 rounds, 1 telephone exchange, 1 stretcher, gunsmith toolbox, crate with medical equipment.	Tarrant-Rushton	LZ "L"
140	PFC Kubaszewski Jan, Pvt Sosiak Józef	2nd Parachute Battalion	2 trailers with ammunition for M-3 mortar	Down Ampney	LZ "L"
141	2nd Lt Heski Stefan, Pvt Kondzior Bronisław, Pvt Kotowski Wacław	2nd Parachute Battalion	2 Jeeps with weapons and ammunition (2 Bren machine guns + ammunition)	Down Ampney	LZ "L"
142	2nd Lt Majewski Kazimierz, Pvt Mikulski Aleksy, strz. Koronka Stanisław	3rd Parachute Battalion	2 Jeeps (load unknown)	Down Ampney	LZ "L"
143	Sgt Sidelnik Włodzimierz, Pvt Lawreszczuk Aleksy	3rd Parachute Battalion	Jeep + trailer (2 *Bren* machine guns, ammunition for M-3 mortars, 2 tripods for Bren)	Down Ampney	LZ "L"
144[9]	Sgt Officer Cadet Hołub Edward, Sgt Nachman Bronisław, PFC Boba Marian	HQ	Jeep + trailer	Down Ampney	The glider pilot lost visual contact with the towplane and crash-landed in Belgium. The soldiers were slightly injured.
145	PFC Kowalewski Henryk, PFC Kruk Jan	Airborne Signals Company	Jeep with R-22 wireless set + trailer., 6 gallons of petrol, tools and spare parts for the Jeep, 1 crate of ammunition for *Sten* submachine gun, 2 telephone sets, signal sheets, sandbags	Down Ampney	LZ "L"
146	kpr. Pilszak Bronisław strz. Żołyniak Bronisław	Airborne Signals Company	Jeep: communication equipment: ASL-3 cable reeler, telephone switch, 2 cable reels, Trailer: R-22 wireless set, 300 W charger, 6 gallons of petrol, crate of rifle ammunition, Jeep spare parts, 2 chest cable reelers, radio technician toolkit, 2 stretchers, 1 *Bren* machine gun+ crate of ammunition, camping tools, tent for telephone, 12 batteries for communication equipment.	Down Ampney	LZ "L"
147[10]	2nd Lt Osuch Władysław[11], Cpl Sobczak Zygfryd Pvt Podlecki Edward (HQ)	Airborne Signals Company/HQ	Jeep with R-22 wireless set+ trailer: wireless set accessories, 6 gallons of petrol, crate of pistol ammunition for Sten submachine gun, spare parts and tools for Jeep, 2 telephone sets, signal sheets, shovels and pickaxes.	Down Ampney	LZ "L"
148	Sgt Łuszczak Marian, Cpl Ohnut Jan	HQ	2 x Jeep	Down Ampney	LZ "L"
149[12]	Sgt Szpetura Błażej, Pvt Jaroszuk Edward, Pvt Marszałek Stanisław	Airborne Medical Company	Jeep No. 1 – no top, windscreen, spare wheel, empty. Jeep No.2 – no top, windscreen and rear seat, with load: four stretchers with straps, food, sterile gauze.	Down Ampney	During the flight over the North Sea, 35 km from Ostend the tow line broke and the glider ditched. The crew were rescued by a British rescue boat[13].

Glider number	Complement	Subunit	Loadout	Airfield of departure	Landing place
150	PFC Michalak Czesław, Pvt Bakun Jan, Pvt Ziemba Bolesław	**Airborne Medical Company**	Jeep No. 1 – no top, windscreen, backseat, empty. Jeep No. 2 – no top, windscreen and rear seat, with load: blood transfusion kit, 2 parachute banners, 2 stretchers with 6 straps, 2 stretcher racks, 8 blankets, one can of sterile gauze.	Down Ampney	LZ "L"
151	PFC Chruściel Tadeusz, Pvt Abramczyk Atanazy	**Airborne Medical Company**	Jeep without top, windscreen, backseat, loaded: 5 stretchers with 4 straps, blood transfusion kit, water sterilization kit, water test kit, blood pressure gauge, 3 blankets, one can of sterile gauze. Trailer No. 1 – haversack with medicaments, 2 tents, 1 thermos, 4 stretchers, 4 stretcher racks, blood transfusion kit, heat lamp, primus, electric lamp, 10 blankets, Trailer **nr 2** – 11 stretchers, dried blood plasma and water, haversack with medicaments, sugar, transfusion stand, 2 stretcher racks, plasma, primus.	Down Ampney	LZ "L"
152[14]	LCpl Drogoś Bronisław, LCpl Grelo Konstanty	**Transport and Supply Company**	Jeep + trailer, ammunition for *Bren* machine gun and PIAT, 2 bicycles, shovels and pickaxes, sleeping bags, masking nets, stretchers, 24-hour food rations.	Down Ampney	After the failure of the Stirling towplane the glider disengaged and force landed near the village of Little Marlow in England, sustaining damage. One of the pilots had both legs broken, the rest escaped unhurt[15]
153	st. strz. Słota Zygmunt strz. Zarychta Jan	**Transport and Supply Company**	Jeep + trailer, ammunition for *Bren* machine gun and PIAT, 2 bicycles, shovels and pickaxes, sleeping bags, masking nets, stretchers, 24-hour food rations.	Down Ampney	LZ "L"
154	W/O Zaremba Piotr, Cpl. Garncarz Tadeusz, PFC Kowalski Józef	**Transport and Supply Company**	Jeep + trailer, ammunition for *Bren* machine gun and PIAT, 2 bicycles, shovels and pickaxes, sleeping bags, masking nets, stretchers, 24-hour food rations.	Down Ampney	Due to a failure of the towplane the plane and glider aborted and returned to base[16].

6   A-J. van Hees, op. cit.,p. 199.
7   *Ibidem*, p. 199.
8   *Ibidem*, s. 198-199; Raport strat w szybowcach, IPMS, sygn. A.V.20/31/21-dok.8; Operation Market Garden. Then and now, red. Karel Margry, London 2002, s. 449.
9   Zestawienie szybowców nr 144 – 148 sporządzono na podstawie: Spad. Komp. Łącz. Zestawienie zrzutu szybowcowego op. MARKET, IPMS, sygn. A.V.20/31/29 – 10; Historia przygotowania do akcji i przebieg operacji "Market", IPMS, sygn. A.V.20/31/40-10; Zestawienie załadowania ludzi i sprzętu Kwatery Głównej wraz z przydzieloną Komp. Łączności, IPMS, sygn. A.V.20/31/31-5, k. 33.
10 Complement determined after: G.F. Cholewczyński, Rozdarty naród, Warsaw 2006, p. 117.
11 2nd Lt Władysław Osuch, intended to travel in this glider had a motorcycle accident on the previous day and stayed in England See: Spad. Komp. Łącz. Zestawienie zrzutu szybowcowego op. MARKET, IPMS, sygn. A.V.20/31/29 – 10, c 18.
12 Para Fidel Ambulance, IPMS, sign. A.V.20/31/24-11. Arie-Jan van Hees wrote that two Polish soldiers were aboard the glider. See: A-J. van Hees, op. cit., p. 193.
13 *Ibidem*, p. 192
14 Aggregate lists state that the Transport and Supply Company had three gliders, numbered 152-154, while the list by Capt. Studziński from 9 October 1944 loads of two gliders are given, but the maker stipulated that at that time he had not complete information to recall the lists of personnel and materiel loaded into the gliders. The errors may concern loads and complements of the gliders. Arie-Jan van Hees states that two Jeeps and two Polish soldiers were loaded aboard he glider No. 154. See: Studziński, Zestawienie załadowania ludzi i sprzętu, IPMS, sign. A.V.20/31/29 – doc.12; A-J. van Hees, op. cit., p. 191. With regard to the glider No. 152, van Hees menions two Jeeps and three soldiers; *Ibidem*, p. 192.
15 *Ibidem*, s. 193.

ANNEX 5

Pattern of loadsheet of materiel and personnel for *Whitley* aircraft[1]

Loadsheet ....(unit, subunit)

Aircraft number and marking	Unit flying	Specification by function, in order of jumping	Armament	Content of containers in the bomb bay									Remarks
				4	5	6	14	15	7		8	9	

---

1   *Nauka przygotowania do działań bojowych* (script for tactical training course for junior officers of the 1st IPB), no year of issue, Military Historic Research Bureau y , sign: V/20/140-II323 44-SKR, appendix 8.

ANNEX 6

Loadout variants of Polish gliders participating in the Operation Market Garden in September 1944

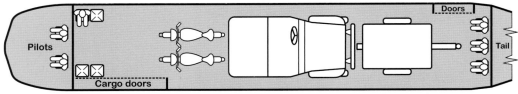

Glider No. 120 of Airborne Anti-tank Squadron

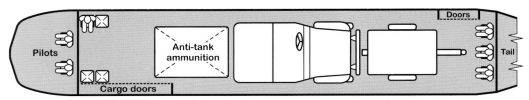

Glider No. 123 of Airborne Anti-tank Squadron

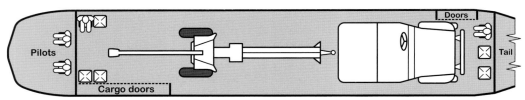

Glider No. 892 of Airborne Anti-tank Squadron

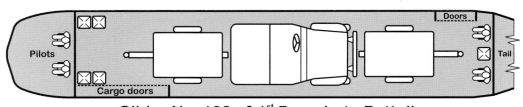

Glider No. 138 of 1st Parachute Battalion

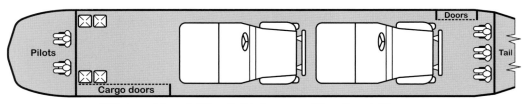

Glider No. 149 of Airborne Medical Company

Formation of aircraft of the 1st Independent Parachute Brigade in flight to Operation Market on 21 September 1944[1].

A 84

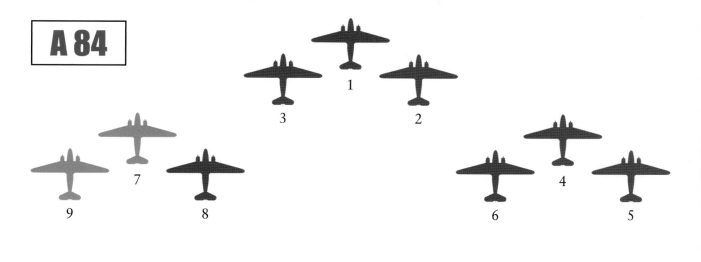

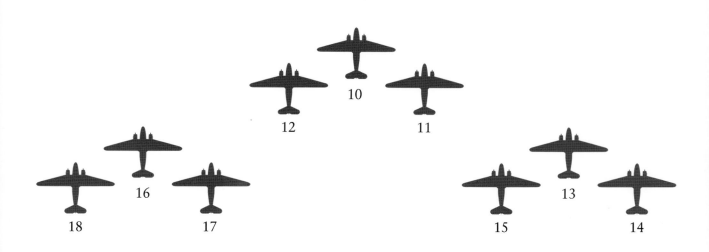

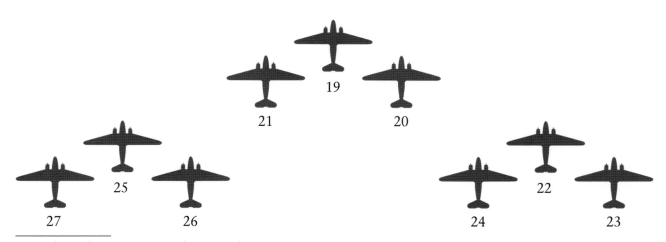

1   Szyk samolotów zrzutu Brygady op. "Market", IPMS, sign. A.V.20/31/28-doc.6, c. 290.

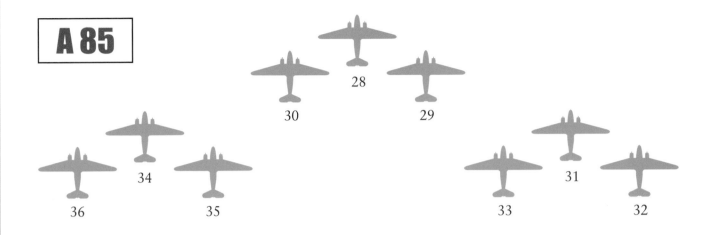

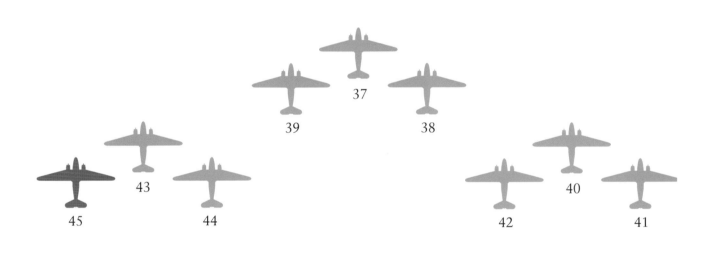

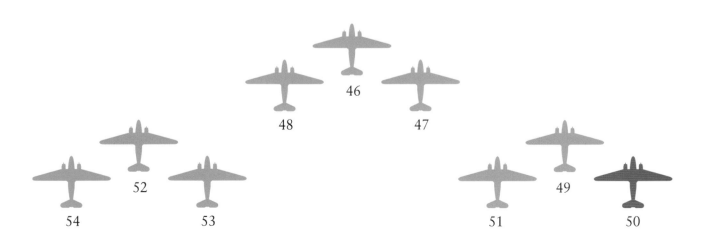

A 86

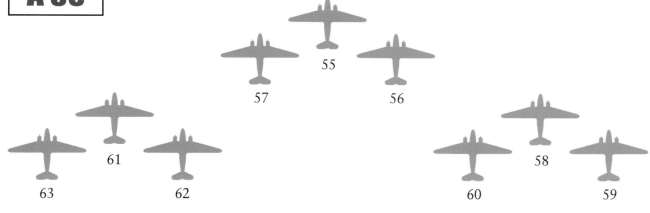

55

57

56

61

63

62

58

60

59

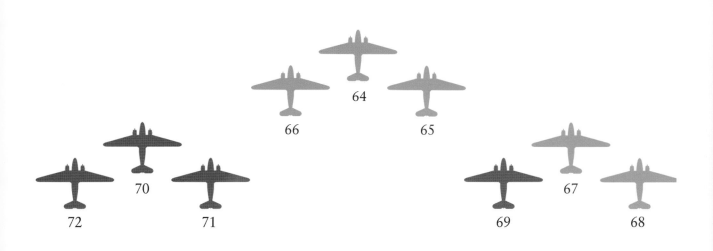

64

66

65

70

72

71

67

69

68

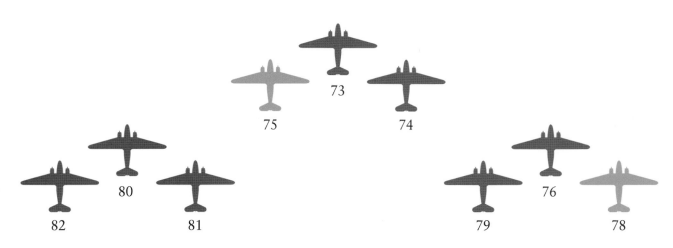

73

75

74

80

82

81

76

79

78

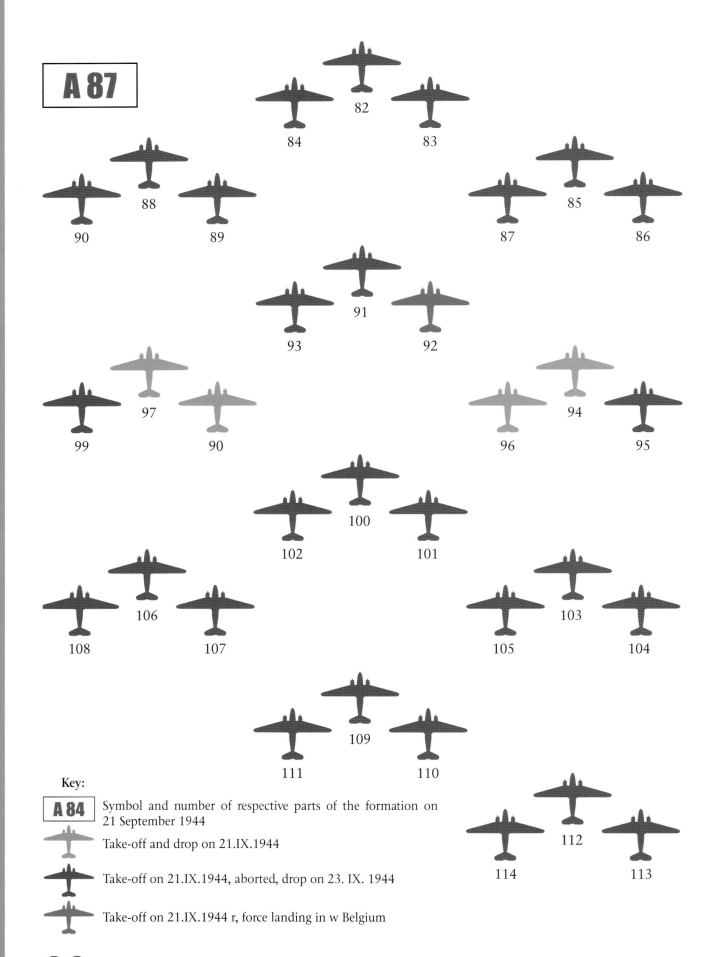

A 87

82
84 83

88
90 89

85
87 86

91
93 92

97
99 90

94
96 95

100
102 101

106
108 107

103
105 104

109
111 110

112
114 113

Key:

A 84   Symbol and number of respective parts of the formation on 21 September 1944

Take-off and drop on 21.IX.1944

Take-off on 21.IX.1944, aborted, drop on 23. IX. 1944

Take-off on 21.IX.1944 r, force landing in w Belgium

92

BIBLIOGRAPHY

Archive sources
Military Historic Research Bureau in Warsaw
Documents and studies on the 1st Independent Parachute Brigade
The Polish Institute and Sikorski Museum in London
Files of the 1st Independent Parachute Brigade
Imagery of the 1st Independent Parachute Brigade

Collections of institutions
• Airborne Museum "Hartenstein" in Oosterbeek (AMH)[1]
• The Polish Institute and Sikorski Museum in London (IPMS)
• Polish Army Museum in Warsaw (MWP)

Private collections
• Jacek Dziędziela – Former Airborne Soldiers Association "Red Berets" (JD)
• Rafał Niedziela (RN)
• Erik van Tilbeurgh (EvT)
• Marek Wroński – *Museum of Tarnowskie Góry Institute* (MIT)
• Piotr Wybraniec– *Lt Col. Adolf Pilch, Silent Unseen Home Army Paratrooper Airborne and Special Forces Museum, Wisła*

Printed sources
Anti-Tank Rifle. Small Arms Training. Volume 1 Pamphlet No 5, Pretoria 1942.
Artillery Ammunition, Washington 1944.
British Explosive Ordnance (Ordnance Pamphlet 1665), Washington 1946.
Carbine Machine Sten 9 mm. Mk.II. General instructions, no place of issue, 1942.
Carbines, Machine, Sten, 9mm. Mks I. II & III. Illustrated identification list, Weedon 1942.
Driver's Handbook for Excelsior "Welbike", Book No. 100/EMI
Handbook of the ML Stokes 3-inch trench mortar equipment, London 1920.
Handbook of the Thompson submachine gun. Model of 1928, model of 1921, New York 1929.
Instrukcja strzelecka. Lekki Karabin Maszynowy, pt.2, Great Brirain 1941.
Instrukcja walki miotaczem przeciwpancernym. Wzór I, Great Britain 1943.
Light Machine Gun. Small Arms Training. Volume 1 Pamphlet No 4, London 1939.
Maintenance manual and instruction book Car, 2-seater, 4×2, Austin Model G/YG. Light Utility 10 H.P, no place of issue, 1944.
Maintenance Manual for Excelsior 98 cc. "Welbike", Book No. 101/EM1
Maintenance Manual for Willys Truck ¼ – Ton 4x4, Ohio 1942
Moździerz 2-calowy, Great Britain 1945.
Nauka przygotowania do działań bojowych (script for tactical training course for junior officers of the 1st IPB), no year and place of issue
Pilot's Flight Operating Instruction. C-47 Airplane, Ohio 1943
Pilot Training Manual for the Skytrain C-47, Washington 1945
Small Arms Training. Pistol .455 inch., vol. 1, no place of issue, 1937.
Sprawozdanie z działalności Ligi Obrony Powietrznej i Przeciwgazowej za rok 1937, Warsaw 1938.
Technical manual. Ordnance maintenance. Thompson submachine gun, cal .45, M1928A1, no place of issue 1942.
Tymczasowy Regulamin Służby Łączności, Warszawa 1920.
¼ – Ton 4x4 Truck (Willys-Overland Model MB and Ford Model GPW), Washington 1944
2 ½-ton 6x6 truck and 2 ½-ton to 5-ton 6x4 truck (Studebaker models US6 and US6x4), Washington 1943
57-MM Gun, M1 (War Department Basic Field Manual FM 23-75), Washington 1944.
75-mm Pack Howitzer M1A1 and Carriage M8, Washington 1948.
Memoirs, diaries, accounts
Polscy spadochroniarze. Pamiętnik żołnierzy, Newtown 1949.
Sosabowski Stanisław, *Droga wiodła ugorem*, London 1967.
Sosabowski Stanisław, *Najkrótszą drogą*, Warszawa 1992.
Stasiak Władysław K., *W locie szumią spadochrony. Wspomnienia żołnierza spod Arnhem*, Warsaw 1991.

---

1   In brackets initials of individuals, organizations and institutions to which the exhibits and copyright to archive photographs belong are given. Photographs not signed are the property of the author or 1st Independent Parachute Brigade Reenactment Group at 12th Detachment of Polish Parachuting Association, Łódź.

Święcicki Marek, *Czerwone Diabły pod Arnhem*, Rome 1945.

Wilk Jan, *Służba wojskowa i wojna 1939-1945. Krótki zarys*, typescript.

Wojdyła Józef, interview with a soldier of the 1st IPB done by the author in 2005.

Studies

British Army Transport 1939-45. Tank Transporters, Recovery Vehicles, Machinery Trucks, red. M.P. Conniford, t.1, Micham Surrey 1972 .

Bishop Kris, *Strielkovoe oruzhe*, no place of issue 2001.

Bouchery Jean, *The British Soldier. From D-Day to VE-Day*, t.2, Paris 1999.

Bystrzycki Przemysław, *Znak Cichociemnych*, Poznań 1991.

Ciepliński Andrzej, Woźniak Ryszard, *Encyklopedia współczesnej broni palnej (od połowy XIX wieku)*, Warsaw 1994.

Chamberlain Peter, Gander Terry, *Anti-Tank Weapons*, no place of issue, 1974.

Cholewczyński George F., *De Polen van Driel*, Naarden 1990.

Cholewczyński George F., *Rozdarty naród*, Warsaw 2006.

Davies Larry, *C-47 Skytrain in action*, Carrollton 1995.

Data Book of Wheeled Vehicles Army Transport 1939-1945, red. David Fletcher, London 1983.

Głębowicz Witold, Matuszewski Roman, Nowakowski Tomasz, *Indywidualna broń strzelecka II wojny światowej*, Warsaw 2000.

Golba Jan, *Służba zdrowia 1.Samodzielnej Brygady Spadochronowej w kampanii na Zachodzie*, typescript, 1946.

Golba Jan, *Służba zdrowia w działaniach 1.Sam. Bryg. Spad. Pod Arnhem-Driel*, a Lecture given on 11.12.1944 w London on Polish Armed Forces Surgeons Convention, typescript, 1944.

Gordon David B., *Equipment of the WWII Tommy*, no place of issue, 2004.

Grant Neil, *The Bren Gun*, Oxford 2013.

Henry Chris, Delf Brian, *British Anti-tank Artillery 1939-45*, Oxford 2004.

Hogg Ian, Adam Rob, *Broń strzelecka. Przewodnik encyklopedyczny*, Poznań 2000.

Hogg Ian, *AliedAtillery of World War Two*, Ramsburry 2001.

Hogg Ian, *Artyleria dwudziestego wieku*, Warszawa 2001.

Haycraft W. C., *The book of the Ariel*, London, no year of issue.

Jane David E., *British military transport*, London 1978.

Kamiński Andrzej A., T. Szczerbicki, *Pojazdy Polskich Sił Zbrojnych na Zachodzie 1939-1947*, Gdańsk 2008.

Kamiński Andrzej A., *Od "Acromy" do "Zwycięzcy"*, t.10, Cracow, no year of issue

Kašeev L.B., *Britanskie vojennye avtomobili 1939-1945*, no year and place of issue

Królikiewicz Tadeusz, *Encyklopedia szybowców wojskowych*, Warsaw 1999

Lucas James, *Pikujące orły. Niemieckie wojska powietrznodesantowe w II wojnie światowej*, Warsaw 2002.

Malinowski Tadeusz, *Sport spadochronowy w Polsce*, Warsaw 1983.

Mała Encyklopedia Wojskowa, red. Jerzy Bordziłowski, vol. 2, Warsaw 1967.

Markert Wojciech, *Na drodze do Arnhem*, Pruszków 2000.

Murgrabia Jerzy, *Symbole wojskowe Polskich Sił Zbrojnych na Zachodzie 1939-1946*, Warsaw 1990.

Norris John, *Infantry Mortars of World War II*, Oxford 2002.

Operation Market Garden. Then and now, red. Karel Margry, London 2002

Orchard Chris, Madden Steve, *British Forces motorcycles 1925-45*, Sutton2006.

Philip Craig, *The World's Great Small Arms*, Hong Kong 2000.

Richard Guy, *World War II Troop Type Parachutes. Allies: U.S., Britain, Russia. An Illustrated Study*, Atglen 2002.

Reynolds E.G.B. , *The Lee-Enfield Rifle*, London 1962.

Rottman Gordon L., *World War II Battlefield Communications*, Oxford 2010.

Rydel Jan, *"Polska okupacja" w północno-zachodnich Niemczech 1945-1948*, Cracow 2000.

Smith W.H.B., Smiths Josef E., *The Book of Rifles*, Harrisburg 1975.

Skibiński Franciszek, *O sztuce wojennej na północno-zachodnim teatrze działań wojennych 1944-1945*, Warsaw 1977.

Thompson Leroy, *Fairbain-Sykes Commando Dagger*, Oxford 2011.

Tucholski Jędrzej, *Cichociemni*, Warsaw 1988.

Tucholski Jędrzej, *Spadochroniarze*, Warsaw 1991.

van Meel Rob, van Meel Monica, *British Airborne Jeeps 1942-1945. Modyfications & Markings*, Tilburg 2002.

van Hees Arie-Jan, *Tugs and Gliders to Arnhem*, Eijsden 2000.

Witkowski Piotr, *Polskie jednostki powietrznodesantowe na Zachodzie*, Warsaw 2009.

Witkowski Piotr, *Walczący orzeł. Barwa i broń 1.Samodzielnej Brygady Spadochronowej 1941-1945*, vol.1, Częstochowa 2014.

Zaloga Steven J., *US Anti-tank Artillery 1941-45*, New York 2005.

Zasieczny Andrzej, *Broń Wojska Polskiego 1939-1945. Wojska lądowe*, Warsaw 2006.

II wojna światowa. Encyklopedia uzbrojenia, red. Andrzej Zasieczny, Warsaw 2000.

Articles, magazines

Erenfeicht L., *Stulecie Jedenastki*, "Strzał" Issue 4, 2004.

Erenfeicht L., *Sten: pistolet maszynowy gentlemanów*, "Strzał" Issue 1, 2008.

Borzemski Wiktor, *Początki szkolenia spadochronowego*, "Spadochron" Issue 113, 1988.

Dyrda Jerzy H., *Udział I Polskiej Samodzielnej Brygady Spadochronowej w desancie wojsk powietrznych w Arnhem we wrześniu 1944 r.*, "Bellona" Issue 10, Łódź 1946.

Skotnicki Mariusz, *1.Samodzielna Brygada Spadochronowa 1942-43*, "Poligon" Issue 2, 2008

Stasiak Władysław, *Uwagi i uzupełnienia do pracy Ryszarda Małaszkiewicza "Bitwa pod Arnhem"*, "WPH" Issue 3, 1957.

Hrehorów Zbigniew, *Ostatni wzlot*, pt.2, "Spadochron", issue 101, 1985.

Źródła internetowe

• Akane, Piotrowicz Wojciech, *Wojskowe scyzoryki brytyjskie w latach 1902-1950*, http://www.dobroni.pl/rekonstrukcje,wojskowe-scyzoryki-brytyjskie-w-latach-1902-1950,7195

• Baker Jon, *Container Light Equipment (CLE)*, http://www.paradata.org.uk/content/container-light-equipment-cle

• Boyd David, *British Mines of the Second World War*, http://www.wwiiequipment.com/index.php?option=com_content&view=article&id=95:british-mines-of-the-second-world-war&catid=47:british&Itemid=59

• *Dropping of solo motor cycle in containers. Report No.A.F.E.E./P.55*,http://www.welbike.co.uk/AFEE%20Report.pdf

• https://360carmuseum.com/en/museum/38/exhibit/2038
• https://archive.org/details/StopThatTankTrianingFilm
• https://bsamuseum.wordpress.com/military-bicycles-in-the-boer-war/
• https://bsamuseum.wordpress.com/1942-ww2-bsa-airborne-bicycle-early-twin-tube-model/
• http://coltautos.com/cagotm200601.htm
• http:Home.earthlink.net/flyboyken/id15.html
• http://milpas.cc/rifles/ZFiles/Enfields/BAYONETS.htm
• http://philippe.chapill.pagesperso-orange.fr/page/container%20MK3.htm
• http://philippe.chapill.pagesperso-orange.fr/page/container%20type%20c.htm
• http://philippe.chapill.pagesperso-orange.fr/page/container%20Type%20H.htm.
• http://philippe.chapill.pagesperso-orange.fr/page/container%20type%20F.htm
• http://philippe.chapill.pagesperso-orange.fr/page/panier%20wickers.htm; dostęp
• http://philippe.chapill.pagesperso-orange.fr/page/parachute%20container.htm
• http://philippe.chapill.pagesperso-orange.fr/page/parachute%20G1.htm
• http://polishscottishheritage.co.uk/?heritage_item=scotland-the-country-of-the-inventors
• https://en.wikipedia.org/wiki/Welbike
• http://www.wftw.nl/wireless18.html
• http://www.armyvehicles.dk/fordwot2.htm
• http://www.army1914-1945.pl/polska/wojska-ladowe-ii-rp/uzbrojenie-wyposazenie-i-sprzet-wojsk-ladowych-ii-rp/pojazdy-bojowe-ii-rp/279-universal-carrier-mk-i-w-psz-na-zachodzie-technika
• http://www.armyvehicles.dk/bdoy.htm
• http://www.armyvehicles.dk/leylandretriever.htm
• http://www.armyvehicles.dk/leylandretriever.htm
• http://www.armyvehicles.dk/fordwot6.htm
• http://www.bernardvanmeurs.nl/index.php?page=cmp-info-en
• http://www.dws-xip.pl/encyklopedia/sam-wot3
• http://www.dws-xip.pl/encyklopedia/vehutilaustin-uk/
• http://www.dws-xip.pl/encyklopedia/vehutilhillman-uk/
• http://www.dws-xip.pl/encyklopedia/vehutilfwd-uk/
• http://www.fairbairnsykesfightingknives.com/the-stories.html
• http://www.henderson-tele.com/vtm/extras/military/field-tels.html
• http://www.infopc.home.pl/whatfor/baza/uzbrojenie_AK.htm
• http://www.irvingq.co.uk/irvingq/history.asp
• http://www.lexpev.nl/fuzesandigniters/unitedkingdom/no247allwaysfuze.html
• http://www.maquetland.com/article-phototheque/5726-dodge-t-110-l-9
• http://www.military-history.org/articles/back-to-the-drawing-board-the-royal-enfield-flying-flea.htm
• http://www.museumoftechnology.org.uk/expand.php?key=519
• http://www.nationaltransportmuseum.org/mv001.html
• http://www.radiomuseum.org/r/mil_gb_wireless_set_no18.html
• http://www.radiomuseum.org/r/mil_gb_wireless_set_no68.html
• http://www.radiomuseum.org/r/mil_gb_wireless_set_no76.html
• http://www.raf.mod.uk/history/armstrongwhitworthwhitley.cfm

• http://www.wftw.nl/wireless18.html
• http://www.wftw.nl/wireless38-2.html
• https://en.wikipedia.org/wiki/Wireless_Set_No._38#/media/File:EMER_TELS_F410-1_-_1.jpg
•   http://www.wwiiequipment.com/index.php?option=com_content&view=article&id=91:british-mortars-of-the-second-world-war&catid=47:british&Itemid=59
• http://www.wheelsofvictory.com/Morris%20commercial%20c8%20P.
• http://www.yesterdays.nl
• Pacut Michał, *Wykrywacz min typu polskiego*, http://www.muzeumwp.pl/emwpaedia/wykrywacz-min-typu-polskiego.php
• Powers Scott, *Historic Sniper Scopes. A comparative Study the No.32 Mk1 (Britain)*, http://www.snipercountry.com/Articles/HistoricSniperScopes_No32Mk1.asp
• Moszner Paweł, *Type X – najlepszy wojenny spadochron*, http://www.dobroni.pl/rekonstrukcje,type-x-najlepszy-wojenny-spadochron,9848
• *WS No.22. Working instruction*, www.vmarsmanuals.co.uk/archive/470_WS22_Working_instructions.pdf
• Wireless Sets No.18. Mark I, Mark II, Mark III and Wireless Sets No.68. Working instructions,
• http://www.vmarsmanuals.co.uk/archive/65_WS18_Working_Instructions.pdf
www.radiomuseum.org/r/mil_gb_wireless_set_no22.html?language_id=6&hl=en&sl=auto&tl=pl&ie=utf-8&oe=utf-8